FRONTIER RANGERS *of* COLONIAL NEW ENGLAND

FROM KING PHILIP'S WAR TO THE AMERICAN REVOLUTION

ANTHONY PHILLIP BLASI

Published by The History Press
An imprint of Arcadia Publishing
Charleston, SC
www.historypress.com

First published 2025

Manufactured in the United States

ISBN 9781467157285

Library of Congress Control Number: 2025931723

Notice: The information in this book is true and complete to the best of our knowledge. It is offered without guarantee on the part of the author or The History Press. The author and The History Press disclaim all liability in connection with the use of this book.

For Louise Davis Blasi

CONTENTS

ACKNOWLEDGEMENTS

This book, being written several centuries after its subjects lived, could not rely on oral histories, as some works on subjects such as the Second World War are able to do. As such, it would have been impossible to tell the stories of the rangers and their families without referring to those who had written about them, both past and present. As such, I am grateful to the local historians then and now who recorded their communities' stories and to those who wrote about the subject of ranging. I would also like to thank Maine's Public Library System and especially Windham Public Library for supplying me with a bounty of books in a speedy manner.

For local historians, I am grateful to Hartley and Nancy Millett of the Acton Massachusetts Historical Society for their offering of materials and support for this project; Sabrina at The Fort at No. 4 Museum for their patience and connections; Lynne Fisk of the Charlestown Historical Society, for their generous help and access to the society's collections—never had I visited such a bountiful and accessible historical society; and Silas Towler for giving me insight into early Ferrisburgh, Vermont, and for his assistance and encouragement. I appreciate the help given to me by Joy and Valerie at the Seth Warner–Rhoda Farrand Chapter, National Society of the Daughters of the American Revolution. And finally, the late Frank Dennis and Dorothy Davis McCall of Erie County provided the spark to my flame with their early genealogical recordings.

For archives, I would like to express my appreciation to those at the archives at Dartmouth University, the State Archives of New York, as well as the vast collections made available online by sites like Ancestry, Family Search, Fold3 and Google Books.

For images, I am grateful to the Yale Center for British Art, the New York Public Library, the Library of Congress and the National Archives. Special thanks go to White Historic Art for the beautiful piece by Pam White that graces the cover of this work.

The final expression of gratitude goes to my family: for my parents, who always supported me; for my wife, who always encouraged me; and all of them for their patience while my mind wandered in and out of the seventeenth- and eighteenth-century woods of New England. Thank you.

INTRODUCTION

There is a clearing visible in the trees that are set back on the northerly side of Rock Landing Road in Ferrisburgh, Vermont. Approaching this clearing, a trail is revealed through the woods, mostly of grass but with bits of slate rock protruding through the surface. Several paths, much narrower than the main, seem to branch off toward nearby Lake Champlain. After nearly one thousand feet, a cemetery is revealed, its old stones facing toward the lake under trees that seem to shade them even in winter, while a tattered American flag sticks out from a notch in a nearby tree.

The cemetery is an old one, and its days of perpetual care have long since passed. Many of the stones have fallen, partially eaten by the earth or even fragmented under years of weathering. But one headstone stands tall and unscarred and seems to loom larger than the others nearby. It bears no elaborate design or messages, simply the names of a husband and wife who were fortunate enough to reach old age.

It seems a fitting stone for a man who in his later years sought a quiet life for his family, perhaps seeking to put the more exciting times of his past behind him. Noah Porter was to his neighbors a hunter and trapper and, like everyone else around, kept a farm for sustenance. He could be irascible at times, but this was not an unfamiliar trait to the frontier folk who lived in western New England in the early nineteenth century.

But before his sunset years, his name was known to many others whose names echo down the years of American, British and Canadian history, people like John Stark, Israel Putnam, Lord George Howe, the Earl of

Loudoun and, perhaps most famously, Robert Rogers—all at times his superior officers and, in the case of Rogers, possibly a friend. For this grave is the resting place of not only an old frontiersman but also an enlisted soldier, a mutineer and an officer in Rogers' Rangers during the French and Indian War; a Patriot in the Revolution; and finally, a material supporter of the U.S. Navy in the War of 1812 who watched one of the battles from that conflict from his homestead just after his eightieth birthday.

Porter was definitely one of the last surviving members of Rogers' Rangers; it is also possible he was the last surviving soldier from the 1758 Battle of Carillon, in which British and provincial forces under General Abercrombie conducted a disastrous frontal assault against the Marquis de Montcalm's dug-in forces. He was also the third generation of his family to serve as a ranger in the New England woods, part of a family that had struggled for existence in the region against the elements, foreign powers and Native American tribes for centuries. In many ways, this family was typical of those early families in the region, producing stories that seem to tell the history of ranging itself.

The use of modern technology has led to a forgetting of just how the New England landscape affected life and warfare in seventeenth- and eighteenth-century New England. Mountains were only surpassed in strategic importance by the passes between them. Rivers and lakes were highways and the backbones of settlements, and portages between them were vital connections. Forests and wilderness could be impassable, disorienting, filled with dangers and a human enemy as well as natural ones such as wolves, bears or lack of any fauna to live off whatsoever, as some rangers would experience. Areas of what we now call New England and New York were then not for the faint of heart; they bred many a hardy man and woman and buried many as well.

A great many people in America and even around the world can claim descent from these early New Englanders and much more rarely from the Indigenous peoples who were there before them (and were nearly driven to extinction by them). The Europeans who came to live and die on this land in the "new world" lived in a markedly different way from their ancestors who sleep in European churchyards. Western Europe and the British Isles had not had real wilderness for centuries, and lands were few and far between that did not belong to nobility. Ignoring the claims to the land by Indigenous peoples, this area offered a fresh start for those who had little in money but a burning desire for improving their families' lives.

The men who would become the early rangers started life as the children of homesteaders at the mercy of all the dangers that came from living on the frontier. They grew up watching their parents do battle with nature and their Indian neighbors, and if they survived to adulthood, they took what they learned to heart either in wisdom or with anger or both. They went on to become hunters, trappers, lumbermen, ferrymen, farmers and artisans on the edges of the map of British Empire. And when their desire to push that edge further and further brought them into repeated conflict with the French and their Native allies, they traded the tools of their occupations for muskets, tomahawks and scalping knives.

A couple of generations later, the men who learned these lessons were able to bring New France to defeat, reduce Native American tribes both enemy and allied to the status of marginal peoples and open up the first northwest frontier to settlement. Less than two decades after that, these same men had to decide whether to remain with the British government they had once fought for or alongside or whether take the greatest gamble of their lives and overthrow it in favor of one of their own makings.

These men were tough in a way that is hard to imagine today. Even those who struggle to put food on the table now have likely never had to track that food through dense forests with death lurking behind every tree. They have not had to worry about who might venture out of those same forests to try to kill them and those they loved and to have loathed and hated those same groups with a rage that was passed on from parent to child. In short, few of us can know just how it felt to be alive in eighteenth-century New England.

These men were of their time, and it is their lives in that time that fascinates us to this day. It is the author's hope the reader will get a better understanding of how these men fought and died for a land of timeless beauty and bounty. This book is not intended to be a general history of Robert Rogers or his rangers. There have been many fine works on that subject through the years; it is possible that there are more books about Rogers' Rangers than there are about the French and Indian War itself. And few can beat Burt Garfield Loescher's detailed volumes or, more recently, John Ross' excellent *War on the Run*.

Nor is this work meant to be a history of European settlement of the Connecticut River Valley or of Lake Champlain. Earlier historians of localities in the region, as well as modern archaeologists, have weaved together histories with detail that is hard to rival even in our modern Information Age. Indeed, it is this author's belief that no one can ever write a more detailed history of Charlestown, New Hampshire, and its wooden walled precursor, the Fort at No. 4., better than Henry Hamilton Saunderson was able to do even in the 1800s.

Rather, this work seeks to tell the stories of the generations of frontiersmen of northwest New England who became masters of wilderness warfare and woodland experts as only Native Americans had been before. These skills and traits came to be embodied in a title that has become a part of early American history and legend: the ranger.

PROLOGUE

Life on the Frontier

Vermont Historian Benjamin Hall wrote, "Compared with the life of the ranger, that of the frontier settler was merely the training school in hardship and endurance." For those who served as snowshoe-men, scouts and rangers in the early eighteenth century, the warfare they practiced was learned from on-the-job training that started in their earliest years. Those who were the most successful had spent most of their lives on the frontier or trained under those that had.[1]

For many in modern America, their next meal is just a trip to the supermarket or gas station away. Should your power go out, your generator may kick on so you can cook your dinner unhindered. Failing that, there is surely a restaurant you can reach on plowed roads. You likely do not have crops or livestock at the mercy of the elements, and the food that you do get may come from several states or even continents away. For even those with limited means, your survival is not usually under threat. As such, life on the New England frontier in the seventeenth and eighteenth centuries would shock the modern person.

If you did not raise enough crops in your harvest or if nature blighted them in some way, there was a real danger that you might not have enough to eat in the winter. During those harsh winters, you might lose your livestock in giant snowdrifts, and while looking for them you might get lost yourself. Wolves and wild cats threatened your animals as well as your family year-round. There was also the danger that your farm might fall prey to French raiders or their Native American allies—that is, if you were

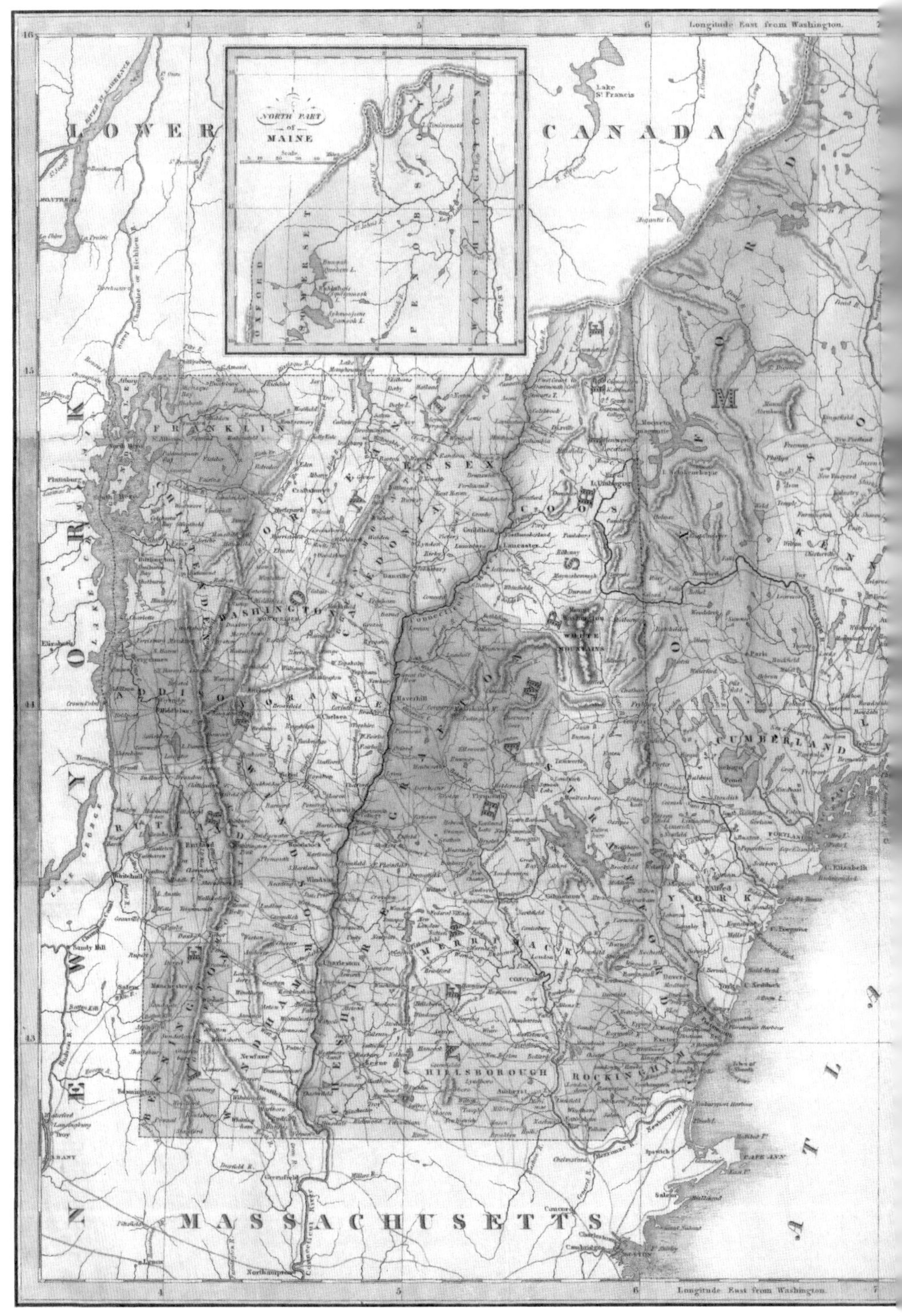
Longitude East from Washington
NORTH PART of MAINE
LOWER
CANADA
Lake St Francis
FRANKLIN
ESSEX
WASHINGTON
ORANGE
ADDISON
WHITE MOUNTAINS
CUMBERLAND
YORK
MERRIMACK
HILLSBOROUGH
ROCKINGHAM
MASSACHUSETTS
PORTLAND
CAPE ANN
BOSTON
Longitude East from Washington

Map of Maine, New Hampshire and Vermont, the past haunts of the colonial rangers. *Courtesy of the Library of Congress, Geography and Map Division.*

lucky enough to not get killed or taken captive and sold into slavery during those raids. These were just some of the dangers of living on the fringes of early New England.

For European settlers, hostile Native Americans were part of the problem; conversely, those tribes felt the same way about the British. The Abenaki in particular had lived and thrived throughout present-day New England, Eastern Canada and the maritime provinces. But since the time of contact with Europeans, they had been devastated by diseases brought by Europeans and were increasingly hemmed in between the settlers of New France moving south and east and those of New England moving north and west. Also, the forests of present-day New Hampshire and Vermont that had been the hunting grounds of the Western Abenaki based at St. Francis, New France, were under threat.[2]

And it was the wilderness that lay between the British and French colonies that became such a battleground. Rene Chartrand, a military historian of this period, vividly described the forests of the region: "Nobody without experience of such thickly forested terrain can truly appreciate its obstacles, accumulated over centuries and millennia: rocky, uneven ground hidden by deep and slippery leaf-mold and entangling brush, and barred every few yards by rotting deadfall trees." For the Native Americans who had lived in the area so long, these were hostile environments that they could traverse and survive in. It was yet to be seen whether the sons of European immigrants would be able to follow suit.[3]

For the hunter and trapper, whether he be of European or Abenaki descent, learning from their surroundings in the woods proved imperative in order to survive them. Signs could be read everywhere, from the behavior of animals to the way trees and moss grew and how they related to the poles and sunlight and what could be learned from the direction of the wind. Different plants and herbs could be used to treat wounds or soothe sores or illnesses. Flowers could furnish material for writing or painting. These all were ways known to Native Americans and would come to be known by the British and French settlers. These were also the basics that one could start with if one was looking to learn the art of warfare in such a harsh environment.

1
KING PHILIP'S WAR

Learning from the Masters

When the first Pilgrims stepped ashore on what they would call Plymouth in Massachusetts Bay, they were but a small group of refugees entering a world almost beyond comprehension. Being strangers in a strange land, they were at first beholden to the friendly Wampanoag people for support. It was not kindness alone that created this alliance but rather several circumstances that led to both parties coming to the table on relatively equal terms.

Native American populations had been devastated by disease, and the Wampanoag found themselves at a disadvantage to other peoples around. Making the Pilgrims their allies could give them an advantage over their neighbors. The Pilgrims, though coming from the wealthiest country in the world, had in many ways to learn how to start agrarian civilization over again in this new land. The Native Americans decided to aid the Englishmen, and together the parties forged the famous origin stories and myths of the birth of New England and the first Thanksgiving.

For the most part, peace prevailed in New England in the decades since the Pilgrims had landed at Plymouth, except for the bloody Pequot War in Connecticut. Such a fact may seem surprising, as much of the next centuries would see the English colonies, and eventually the United States, almost constantly at war with the Indigenous peoples of North America. However, though open warfare was not occurring at that point, the rapid growth of the colonies and the more belligerent stance they took to the Natives neighboring them eventually made war inevitable.

The peace ended with King Philip's War of 1675–76, in which several southern New England tribes combined their efforts and nearly pushed the English colonists into the sea. The allied tribes were led nominally by Metacomet, known to White settlers under the Christian name of King Philip. The son of Massasoit (meaning "great sachem or chief") Ousamequin who had welcomed the pilgrims to Plymouth, his heir now looked to save his land from their children and grandchildren, having realized too late that they would not be content with what they already had. His Wampanoag tribe was joined by several other confederacies and tribes, though each often had its own motives for getting involved.[4]

At first, the war went badly for the English colonists. Settlements throughout Massachusetts, Rhode Island and other parts of New England were sacked, and their inhabitants were killed, kidnapped or often left homeless. Militia units bumbled into ambushes that became massacres. One of those killed was Sergeant Samuel Wright, who died in the defense of Northfield, Massachusetts. The Wright family came from England to Massachusetts with the Puritan migration. The first Samuel Wright who brought his family to America was a settler of Springfield, Agawam and finally Northampton, where he was a deacon of the church. He had many children, including Samuel Jr., who moved to Northfield with his family a couple of years before the war. The second Samuel is said to have had eight children, from Benjamin, who was the first in his line born in America, to Benoni, who was born ten days after his father was killed.[5]

Samuel likely had no military experience other than drilling with the local militia. He had come from the old world to the new at a time of peace and, like other New Englanders, was unprepared for a frontier war or any kind for that matter. His family spent the rest of the war and the years that followed picking up the pieces. But his sons, especially Benjamin, eventually became some of foremost frontier warriors of Massachusetts and the region in general.

The Native American tribes achieved great successes against their enemies, mounting raids and surprise attacks that shocked Europeans, who had mostly known "gentlemanly" warfare, with their brutality. Had they more warriors and supplies, they might have reclaimed all New England and would certainly have changed the course of world history. But their weakness in numbers began to tell, and the English militia and their Indian allies gained the upper hand, going on the offensive with just as much brutal force. As his own allies were destroyed or surrendered, Metacomet was soon forced to go into hiding.

THE DEATH OF KING PHILIP

The mission of finding and bringing Metacomet to justice proved in many ways to be one of the earliest examples of ranging in New England and its genesis in western warfare in general. It was a colonist named Benjamin Church who was selected to lead this quest. Church was originally from the Plymouth colony, but at the commencement of hostilities, he was living in what is now Rhode Island. He was the only European settler in his area, meaning that his prosperity and survival depended on cordial relations with his Native American neighbors. His respect for their ways led him to develop a broader perspective, learning how to navigate the forests and swamps of southern New England as the Indigenous peoples had for generations. These skills would serve the search he was charged with well.

Church formed a combined force of Sakonnet warriors and English militiamen to hunt for Metacomet along the borderlands of Massachusetts and Rhode Island. The knowledge of the terrain Church's Sakonnet warriors possessed proved invaluable and allowed them and the Englishmen to act as a mobile scouting and special operations force, the definition of what would later be known as ranging.

Benjamin Church, the first true ranger active on the New England frontier. *Courtesy of the Miriam and Ira D. Wallach Division of Art, Prints and Photographs: Print Collection, New York Public Library.*

Church's force combed the area where the chief was said to be and found little but received the breakthrough they had been looking for at Aquidneck Island. There, a Wampanoag who had fled from Metacomet after the latter had allegedly killed his brother revealed his former leader's hiding place to Church; he then led the force to Mount Hope in was it present-day Bristol, Rhode Island. Church's men surrounded the camp and began to advance on it. A random encounter led to a premature volley by the English and Sakonnet warriors, and

The crumpled body of Metacomet, moments after being killed by John Alderman, a Wampanoag ranger. *Courtesy of the Miriam and Ira D. Wallach Division of Art, Prints and Photographs: Print Collection, New York Public Library.*

though five of Metacomet's men were killed, he escaped along with his top commander, Anawan.

Metacomet did not get far, coming upon an Englishman and Sakonnet warrior blocking his path. The Englishman missed, but the Sakonnet, called Alderman, did not. The former Native American leader fell face-first into the swamp with a wound to the chest, never to rise again. Church, holding to the belief that Metacomet had been a traitor to the English King Charles II, had the body pulled from the mud, beheaded and then quartered, as traitors were dealt with back in England. The dead leader's hand was given to Alderman as a trophy for doing the deed.

Metacomet was dead, but Anawan had escaped and remained at-large. Eventually, it was learned that he was hiding near a swamp near what is present-day Rehoboth, Massachusetts. Church's task force set out from Plymouth and came to the place. Following stealthily behind two Native Americans entering the camp, they quickly moved in and disarmed all the warriors, capturing them and Anawan. The latter was sent to Plymouth, where he was tried and executed.

The Native Americans who fought the English paid a heavy price in defeat. Those who survived execution or being sold to slavery in the Caribbean were left as stateless persons, their land taken from them. Benjamin Church became New England's premier frontier fighter for the next few decades and later led expeditions to Maine and the Atlantic provinces of Canada during King William's and Queen Anne's Wars.[6]

One of the first uses of the tactic of ranging in New England had paid off. While others refined and honed the fighting style, Church's use of a mixed English and Native American force that operated in dense, enemy-infested terrain set a pattern for later operations. Numbers and firepower aside, the English had benefited from including Native Americans in their first great war against other Native Americans, both in using and learning from their skill sets and playing the different tribes off one another.

2

KING WILLIAM'S WAR

New France's War of Terror

As New France and New England expanded from their river and coastal birthplaces, North America fast became a smaller place. It was not long before these frontiers of European kingdoms soon met either their counterparts or the other's allied Native American peoples. Colonial expansion along with a war between the kingdoms of England and France back in Europe led to King William's War in the upper part of North America, part of the Nine Years' War that began in Europe in the spring of 1688.

Going into the war heavily outnumbered and with reinforcements from France unlikely, Count Frontenac, governor of New France, realized a new strategy was needed to combat the English colonies. Understanding that great offensives and occupation of territory in New England were not feasible, he decided his best course of action was to conduct raids using his few troops, Canadian militia and their Native American allies (most prominently the Wabanaki people) to conduct raids on English settlements.[7]

At this time, European wars were waged by clashes of large armies in the field and sieges of fortifications. Frontenac's way of war was in some ways one of terror. New England and parts of New York saw frontier settlements burned, civilians killed or kidnapped and crops destroyed, echoing the kind of raids seen in King Philip's War. A panicked New England militia force was forced to respond, only to find the raiders had slipped away. Rather than claiming land or seeking a decisive clash of arms, this type of warfare used terror as its main weapon.[8]

The most infamous raid to emerge from this conflict was one launched on a New York community, rather than one in New England. A force of about two hundred Canadians and Native Americans left Montreal, Quebec, to raid Albany, New York. Believing Albany's defenses too formidable, they decided to attack Schenectady instead. The settlement was taken by surprise, leaving about sixty dead and nearly thirty prisoners brought on a forced march to Canada. Besides the cost in lives and property, this attack struck fear into the hearts of English settlers.[9]

Politically, Frontenac might have tried to divide the English colonies, but by choosing a raiding strategy, he further united them. They began to combine efforts against their northern neighbor, viewing the complete defeat of New France as their best guarantee of safety. During King William's War, an attempt was even made to lay siege to Quebec, though it was unsuccessful. Still, it was raids from New France against the ever-expanding New England colonies that characterized frontier warfare for over half of the eighteenth century and kept the British and French colonies on a collision course from which only one could emerge.[10]

3

QUEEN ANNE'S WAR

Carnage on the Connecticut

Conflict in Europe in the early 1700s over which royal family would inherit the throne of Spain led to the War of the Spanish Succession, spilling over into the American colonies as Queen Anne's War. The memories of French raids in the last war were still fresh in the minds of colonial officials from both empires, and the pattern of warfare resumed in much the same way in the spring of 1702.

Going forward, New England had a stalwart enemy and New France a strong ally in the Abenaki tribe. Originally based in Maine and the Connecticut River Valley, the Abenaki had been displaced by wars and ever-expanding English settlements, finding homes with French missions at Bécancour and St. Francis. The Penacook of the Merrimack River Valley and the Western Abenaki who had lived along the Connecticut River had retreated to these places as well, and the latter also established a base at Missisquoi on Lake Champlain. With their lands being taken at an ever-faster pace, they had little to lose in siding with the French against their common enemy.

In the winter of 1704, a force of over two hundred French, Caughnawaga and Abenaki warriors raided the Connecticut River Valley town of Deerfield, Massachusetts, taking the town by surprise late on March 10. Using snowdrifts, they were able to get over the wooden walls and overwhelm the twenty militiamen stationed within.

The "Last Remaining House of the Deerfield Massacre," as it appeared in 1859. It is typical of the early garrison houses of the region. *Courtesy of the Miriam and Ira D. Wallach Division of Art, Prints and Photographs: Print Collection, New York Public Library.*

The town was burned, somewhere between forty and fifty settlers were killed and over one hundred were taken captive; the Massachusetts soldiers stationed nearby were unable to follow due to a lack of snowshoes. Racing against starvation and winter weather back to New France, many captives died along the journey as well, with those surviving being sold only to await a possible parole.[11]

Snowshoeing companies of armed settlers were formed to mount search-and-destroy missions but met with little success. Years later, in 1709, Captain Benjamin Wright of Northampton finally led a force of fifteen settlers and two Native Americans deep into Abenaki territory. Near the northern end of Lake Champlain, they clashed with a Franco-Native force, killing and scalping two of the enemy. They fought another battle on the return journey and, after realizing they had been discovered and were out of their depth, beat a hasty retreat back to Massachusetts. The provincial government awarded them bounty money for killing six to eight Native Americans.[12]

The act of scalping is one that, understandably, remains controversial to this day, being associated with so-called Indian raids and frontier warfare in what would become the United States in general. In his *History of Eastern Vermont*, Benjamin Hall wrote that "the government of Massachusetts had offered a large bounty for every 'Indian killed or captured,' and to gain this reward, did these ranging parties engage in what were commonly known at the time as 'scalping designs.'" Basically, this was state-supported bounty hunting.[13]

The process was originally used by the Iroquois but spread along with European settlements in the new world, it being said that "as the settler spread, so did scalping." Provincial governments offered bounties to their Native American allies and later ranging companies to get proof of their successful raids and skirmishes, and it was sometimes used as a currency all its own. It was a brutal practice for a brutal time but not one that should be blamed on Native Americans alone.[14]

In addition to scalping as proof of success for scouting missions by rangers in the decades preceding and into the French and Indian War, those leaders who were literate often carried journals documenting their missions, showing that even if they did not locate an enemy, they at least tried to do so. These journals also helped map the frontier by recording trails and routes taken and to this day give historians insight into the tactics and experiences of those early New England rangers.

Things could have gone better for Wright's expedition, but he was not put off. In a letter to the governor of Massachusetts, Wright wrote the following:

> *With submission and under correction, I offer my services to ye excellency, if that in wisdom you send forces to Canada from our posts by land that "here I am, send me." This year I have done service, and hope I may again, not that I would trouble your excellency, but am willing to go. Not else, but in duty I subscribe myself: Ye Excellency's most humble servant, Benjamin Wright.*[15]

With an eagerness such as this, and with the loss of his father to Native American raiders, it is no wonder that Wright achieved such fame as an "Indian fighter." He passed on his skills, as well as his harsh views on the northern neighbors of New England, to his family members, especially his children and grandchildren.

A few years later, peace was achieved in Europe and followed in North America. One of the more famous results of this war was the number of unemployed seamen in the Caribbean who turned to piracy. In New England, it simply meant a few years' pause before the next conflict between settlers and Native Americans, though the next time would be more of a neighbors' argument than a clash of empires.

4
DUMMER'S WAR

Grey Lock versus Massachusetts

Into this violent and unforgiving frontier came the Porter family. Coming from England and being founders of Farmington, Connecticut, the family then made their way up the Connecticut River Valley into Massachusetts. It was there, possibly in Northampton, that James Porter was born in the late 1690s, and he and his sons soon became some of the most active participants in frontier warfare.[16]

James Porter served at Northfield during Dummer's War, also known as Father Rale's War, named for the acting governor of Massachusetts, William Dummer, whose state (which at that time included most of what is now Maine) was the primary combatant against the New England Wabanaki. The war took place mostly in what is present-day Maine but also in the Connecticut River Valley of Massachusetts, New Hampshire and Vermont, which were under threat from the Abenakis under the formidable Chief Grey Lock. Dummer's War is often called Grey Lock's War in this region of New England. This was a war between the English province and Native Americans, rather than one between England and France.[17]

From July to November 1722, Porter served with Captain Samuel Barnard's Company from Deerfield and Northampton, which was serving in the defense of Northfield. Despite peace offering and gifts from Governor Dummer, the town was raided in the summer of 1723, resulting in several deaths. This was then followed with a raid on a family of workers in a meadow near Rutland, in which two were killed and a few others captured, including a young Phineas Stevens (who will be heard from again in the history of this region, once redeemed from captivity).[18]

Northfield was attacked again that fall, with several killed, wounded or abducted to Canada. At this time, James Porter was apparently garrisoned with the family of Benjamin Wright, one of the most famous Indian fighters of the area. Wright had proposed leading an expedition in this war, but his request went unanswered; instead, a blockhouse was

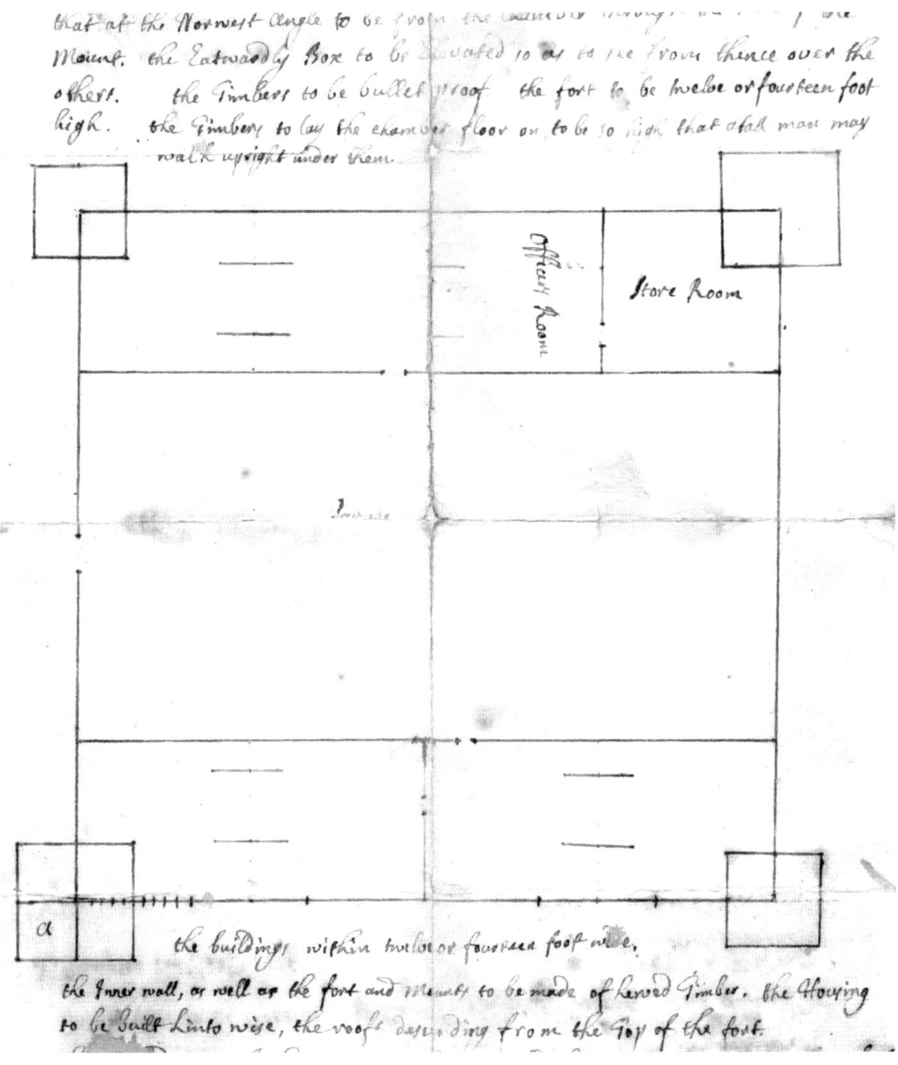

Plan of Fort Dummer as drawn by Colonel Thomas Stoddard. Forts like these were vital in holding the Connecticut River Valley. *Courtesy of Wikipedia.*

built near present-day Brattleboro, Vermont, called Fort Dummer. It was typical of the forts of the region, with a wooden stockade surrounding a small number of buildings inside connected by thick wooden walls. Such a structure would not stand up well to artillery fire, but it had only to withstand sniping and charges with tomahawks.

In November 1723, Porter joined Captain Joseph Kellogg's company in Northfield, serving in the unit until the fall of 1724. Captain Wright finally led his expedition in the summer of 1725, heading up the Connecticut to the mouth of the Wells River and from there northwest through the woods to Lake Champlain. His objective was to assault Grey Lock's base at Missisquoi, but this was fated to never be taken by the English. Wright and his men had to head home due to fatigue and dwindling provisions.[19]

In 1725, Porter joined Captain Thomas Wells of Deerfield on a ranging expedition up the Connecticut River. On their return trip, their canoe went over a set of falls (possibly Bellows Falls) and three men drowned in the rapids. Porter, along with Lieutenant Joseph Clesson and Samuel Harmon, came out of the water with "great difficulty." His petition to the government of Massachusetts Bay lists him as having lost his gun, valued at five pounds, and his blanket and other "accoutrements fitted for such an expedition," also valued at five pounds.[20]

While staying in the Wright house, James Porter apparently fell in love with one of the daughters, likely marrying Experience Wright in the mid-1720s. They had seven children, Mary, James, Sarah, William, Noah and two Nathans, who apparently both died young. Unfortunately, little is known of the daughters, but the sons learned from their family how to survive in the New England wilderness and eventually became some of the region's toughest fighters.[21]

Frustrated in the western theater, the English fared much better in present-day Maine. The Native American settlement at Norridgewock was destroyed, and Father Rale, a purported instigator of raids on English settlements, was killed in the action. Most famously, a ranging company under Jonathan Lovewell eliminated Chief Paugus at Pequawket (now Fryeburg, Maine), though Lovewell himself was killed in the bloody encounter. The Western Abenaki and their allies eventually made peace with Massachusetts in 1727.[22]

Through the next two decades, English settlers moved farther up the Connecticut River past Fort Dummer and including the Great Meadow (present-day Putney, Vermont), purchasing lands from the Schaghticoke people, among others. The farthest settlement up the river, at Plantation

No. 4, was begun in 1740 by the Farnsworth brothers, David, Samuel and Stephen, though only the latter remained beyond the founding of the settlement. By about 1744, there lived about nine or ten families who were brave enough to reside so far north of the comparative safety of other Massachusetts towns and garrisons, including the family of Phineas Stevens. In November 1743, the townsfolk voted to construct a fortress to protect themselves from attack by the French or the Abenaki.[23]

Unlike Fort Dummer, the cost and labor of building this structure was not covered by Massachusetts Bay but by the settlers themselves. Legend states that it was constructed under the supervision of Colonel John Stoddard of Northampton, Massachusetts, who had also designed the blockhouse at Fort Dummer. Nearly an acre in size, it was described by town historian Henry Hamilton Saunderson as being "about the size of Fort Dummer, which was 180 feet on a side; it being built in the form of a square. The walls were made of large, squared timbers laid horizontally one above the other, and locked together at the angles in the manner of a log cabin."[24]

Chamberlain & Paugus at Lovewell's Fight. While Benjamin Wright met with frustration in the west, Lovewell's rangers achieved a great victory in present-day Maine. *Courtesy of the Miriam and Ira D. Wallach Division of Art, Prints and Photographs: Print Collection, New York Public Library.*

A reconstruction of the Fort at No. 4., a museum dedicated to Charlestown, New Hampshire's colonial past. *Courtesy of John Phelan and Wikipedia.*

There were dwelling houses inside the fort called province houses, and these were built against the walls of the structure. While Fort Dummer was stockaded (a wall of tall, pointed logs sticking out from the ground and forming a defensive wall) all around it, No. 4. had a stockade only on the north side (facing New France), but it was twelve feet high. It seems that this was later extended around the entire fort. This work was completed just in time, as it was needed to help the settlement face the next colonial war with New France and the colony's Native American allies.[25]

5

KING GEORGE'S WAR

Chasing Shadows

In the spring of 1744, war in Europe broke out once more after the death of Holy Roman Emperor Charles VI and the period of instability that ensued. In the usual European pattern, one kingdom invaded another, and their alliances soon set much of the continent aflame, this time resulting in the War of the Austrian Succession. In a conflict that pitted Great Britain and France against each other once again, their colonies in America joined in the struggle in what would be known in New England as King George's War.[26]

Building on earlier success in the past wars, some of the colonies formed companies of "snowshoe men" who were able to man frontier garrisons as well as patrol for and seek out raiding parties from New France. Governor William Shirley placed a bounty of one hundred pounds on each Native American scalp taken, a kind offer issued neither for the first nor the last time.[27] In time, these companies came to be called ranging companies and their men *rangers*, a term used in old England to describe "a far traveling forester or borderer." The outposts of empire that these men garrisoned and operated from included Fort Massachusetts along the Hoosac River, on the state's western border near Albany; Fort Dummer; a small structure at the Great Meadow; and the northernmost on the Connecticut, the Fort at No. 4.[28]

In 1745, the capture of the famed fortress of Louisbourg in Nova Scotia by New Englanders prompted New France to hit the northwest frontier of the British colonies especially hard. Massachusetts sought to prepare for assaults by the French and their Wabanaki allies. Initially, Massachusetts had trouble garrisoning these forts, with Dummer being under strength and No. 4 containing only the settlers living there. By the summer of 1745, war had come to the area when an English settler was killed at the Great Meadow. That fall, the Great Meadow was attacked again with even greater intensity. For even the hearty settlers in the area, things were becoming far too dangerous.[29]

SIEGE OF FORT AT NO. 4

By the spring of 1746, the Fort at No. 4 was proving a dangerous place to be. Settlers there fought a number of skirmishes with the Abenaki, with casualties on both sides and settlers like Obadiah Sartwell being taken captive to Quebec. By now, the English had changed the focus of their vexation from Missisquoi to St. Francis, a Catholicized Native American town on the Richelieu River. The fact that this town was slightly farther away from them gave the settlers no comfort and must have only added to their fear of attacks. In June, a group of settlers led by Phineas Stevens repulsed another attack, and the Abenaki raided farther south as well.[30]

As the settlers were unable to leave the walls of the fort to work the cattle or a harvest, they were unprepared to spend the winter there and had to depart downriver. Captain Stevens petitioned Governor Shirley to be allowed to re-garrison the New Hampshire forts and was ordered to take a company of about thirty men with him to secure No. 4. in April 1747. Their arrival could not have been timelier, as a Franco-Abenaki force about four hundred men strong was on its way to seize and possibly destroy the settlement.[31]

Just a few days after the arrival of Stevens' force, the dogs at the fort began to act uneasy and barked incessantly. Being frontiersmen, they knew that an uneasy dog did not bode well, and the gate was guarded closely. One man went out beyond the walls to see what was disturbing the dogs. While he was trying to calm the animals, a party of Abenaki warriors stood up from behind a log and fired their pieces. The man was slightly wounded but made it back to the gate.[32]

Their ambush discovered, the warriors began to fire at the fort from all sides and set fire to structures outside the fort, a tactic helped by the dry, windy conditions at the time. Stevens wrote to Governor Shirley that "suddenly we were entirely surrounded by fire." The fort was fired on through the next day, with the barrage stopping only past sunset. The garrison was prevented from eating or sleeping but maintained good morale throughout the ordeal. The warriors then set up a mobile barricade to get close to the fort and set the walls on fire, but they first asked for a ceasefire until a morning parley.[33]

The French and Americans agreed to meet in the no-man's-land outside the fort. The French officer said his force of four hundred was twice that number and that prisoners would be treated humanely and taken to Montreal, but if Stevens did not surrender, the garrison would likely be massacred. Stevens simply replied, "My men are not afraid to die," and the siege continued as it had before.[34]

Three days after the attack began, the French sought to parley once again. This time they said they would lift the siege and return to New France if the garrison would sell them supplies to see them through the journey. Stevens replied that he would not sell the supplies for money but would exchange them for prisoners. Hearing this, the French fired some potshots at the fort and departed, having failed to take the Fort at No. 4.[35]

If the French had any kind of artillery, things would have been quite different, but such sieges would not be seen until the next war. The garrison of thirty men under Stevens had survived a siege by a force at least twice their number. Hearing of Stevens' brave stand, Commodore Sir Charles Knowles of the Royal Navy had a fine sword made and presented to Stevens. To return the honor, the settlement at No. 4 and its surroundings was named Charlestown and in 1753 was incorporated into the province of New Hampshire.[36]

"To Catch Indians"

Despite the success of withstanding the siege, No. 4 was not done witnessing conflict. Multiple skirmishes occurred through the end of 1747 and into 1748.[37] James Porter and his son James Jr. enlisted in Captain Phineas Stevens' company on March 1, 1748, with their objective being to "to catch Indians." In the early part of June, James Porter Jr., William Heywood and two others marched to Fort Dummer and back. While they were gone, another skirmish on snowshoes occurred in which the Abenaki won the day.[38]

This is also the last recorded mention of James Porter the elder. It is likely he died sometime after 1751, as his last date of service with Captain Stevens was on June 21, 1751. As he lived in a frontier town, it is possible his death was not recorded in official records and he was buried in an unmarked grave, both due to the lack of a stone carver and to keep his grave from being disturbed if the fort were attacked again. His sons went on to become settlers of Charlestown.[39]

For the first part of 1748, James' second son, William, served under Captains Josiah and Jonathan Willard at Fort Dummer, where, fortunately for the militia, they did not see any action. William joined his father and brother in serving under Phineas Stevens in October of the same year and continued to serve in the unit into the next decade.[40]

That May, Stevens' men joined with those of Captains Humphrey Hobbs (who would later serve in Rogers' Rangers) and Eleazer Melvin on an expedition through the Green Mountains to Otter Creek. Melvin's men broke off and headed toward Fort St. Frederic (present-day Crown Point, New York) and fired on a party of Native Americans in canoes. On their way home, Melvin was ambushed and lost about a third of his force before reaching Fort Dummer. Stevens and Hobbs failed to encounter any enemies. Hobbs was ambushed on another expedition, but his men were able to acquit themselves better than Melvin's and claim the skirmish as a victory.[41]

Military actions continued at No. 4 on June 20, 1748, when Native Americans again skirmished with the garrison. Heywood wrote in his journal that

> *about 3 o'clock the Indians fired on Obadiah Sartwell and Enos Stevens as they were harrowing corn, killed Sartwell and took Enos and killed the horse. We instantly fired 2 alarms with small arms and fired the great gun, to alarm James Porter, Lt. Willard and two sons who were working in the meadow. They heard the guns and took off for Fort Dummer. I set off to carry news. The next day we got to Fort Dummer about 9 o'clock in the morning, found the runaways there.*

Porter and his companions were fortunate to be close to the safety of Fort Dummer when the raid occurred, while clearly Sartwell and Stevens, who was the son of Captain Phineas, were not as lucky, though Stevens was later redeemed from captivity.[42]

The peace treaty of Aix-La-Chapelle signed in the autumn of 1748 notwithstanding, the garrison of the Fort at No. 4. still stood ready. James and William Porter were both listed in Captain Stevens' company in 1750. The English scouting companies had not performed well in this war, with historian Colin Calloway writing, "The English rarely obtained an Indian scalp, even the Fort at No. 4., where the fighting was fiercest, because the men would not venture out after the enemy." A feeling of animosity remained toward the Native Americans at St. Francis, and that enmity would bear fruit in a few years with the coming of the next colonial conflict, one in which the frontiersmen of New England performed much better.[43]

6
THE FRENCH AND INDIAN WAR, 1754–57

Bushwacked

War in the Wilderness

In the 1750s, a fragile peace existed in the frontier between New France, the Abenaki lands and New England. Phineas Stevens traded with Native Americans at St. Francis and also participated in prisoner exchanges from raids in the past war. Stevens himself said "that were it not for ye French it would be for easy to live at peace with ye Indians." Though he failed to consider the English hunger for land, he was correct about the future regarding the French at least. When war broke out again, it came from out west in addition to their own locale and was brought about by the distant European kingdoms rather than the neighbors of the northern territories.[44]

North America, though vast, was not big enough for France and Great Britain to share. The former held the colonies of New France and Louisiana, while the latter held colonies clustered around the East Coast of the continent. The British colonies sought westward expansion while the French looked to link their northern and southern dominions through the same area, a move that would fence in the British. Central to this border dispute was the forks of the Ohio, found in present-day Pittsburgh, Pennsylvania. It is here that the Allegheny, Monongahela and Ohio Rivers meet; the Ohio flows to the Mississippi River, which flows down to Louisiana and the Gulf of Mexico. And it is here that a conflict that many have called the world's first "world war" began.

The French began moving south from present-day Lake Erie, building Forts Presque Isle and Fort LeBoeuf. These posts were built to help in trading with the Native American tribes nearby and promoting French settlement in the region. Viewing these lands as part of their own claims, the Virginians under Governor Robert Dinwiddie dispatched a young militia officer named George Washington to ask the French to vacate this area. The French politely told the young Washington that they were there to stay.

Washington, later the first president of the United States, was eulogized as being "first in war, first in peace, and first in the hearts of his countrymen." The first segment of that line holds true when describing the start of the French and Indian War in North America. Having failed to expel the French, he became involved in an armed border conflict that reached its climax at the Battle of Jumonville Glen, in which Jumonville, commander of the Franco-Canadian force ambushed by Washington, was killed. Whether he died in the skirmish or was murdered afterward is debated to this day, and the rumors of this alleged assassination helped light the spark that set both Europe and North America ablaze.

The war that started in Western Pennsylvania quickly spread to the borderlands between New France and the Northeast colonies, particularly New Hampshire, Massachusetts and New York, and primarily in the Champlain valley. This area consisting of Lake Champlain, Lake George and the surrounding wilds were the scene of much fighting over the next few years.

Forming a natural route between Quebec and Albany, New York, this area came to be known by Native Americans as the "great warpath" and was about two hundred miles from Albany to Montreal.[45] In order to make the journey from one location to the other, one might sail southwest from Quebec City along the St. Lawrence. From there, one would head south along the Richelieu River into Lake Champlain. After a portage (carrying boats overland from one body of water to the next) at Carillon (Ticonderoga to the British) to Lake George, one could then make a comparatively brief overland journey to the Hudson River, reaching Albany on the west bank and eventually New York City at its southernmost point.

For white settlers, the Champlain Valley remained largely a wilderness, its forests full of the dangers of nature and hostile European and Native American forces. But by traveling via canoe, bateau or even a small ship through these waterways, one could greatly reduce the time and dangers of the journey from the heart of New France deep into the British colonies. It is this convenience that gave the Champlain Valley its vital military

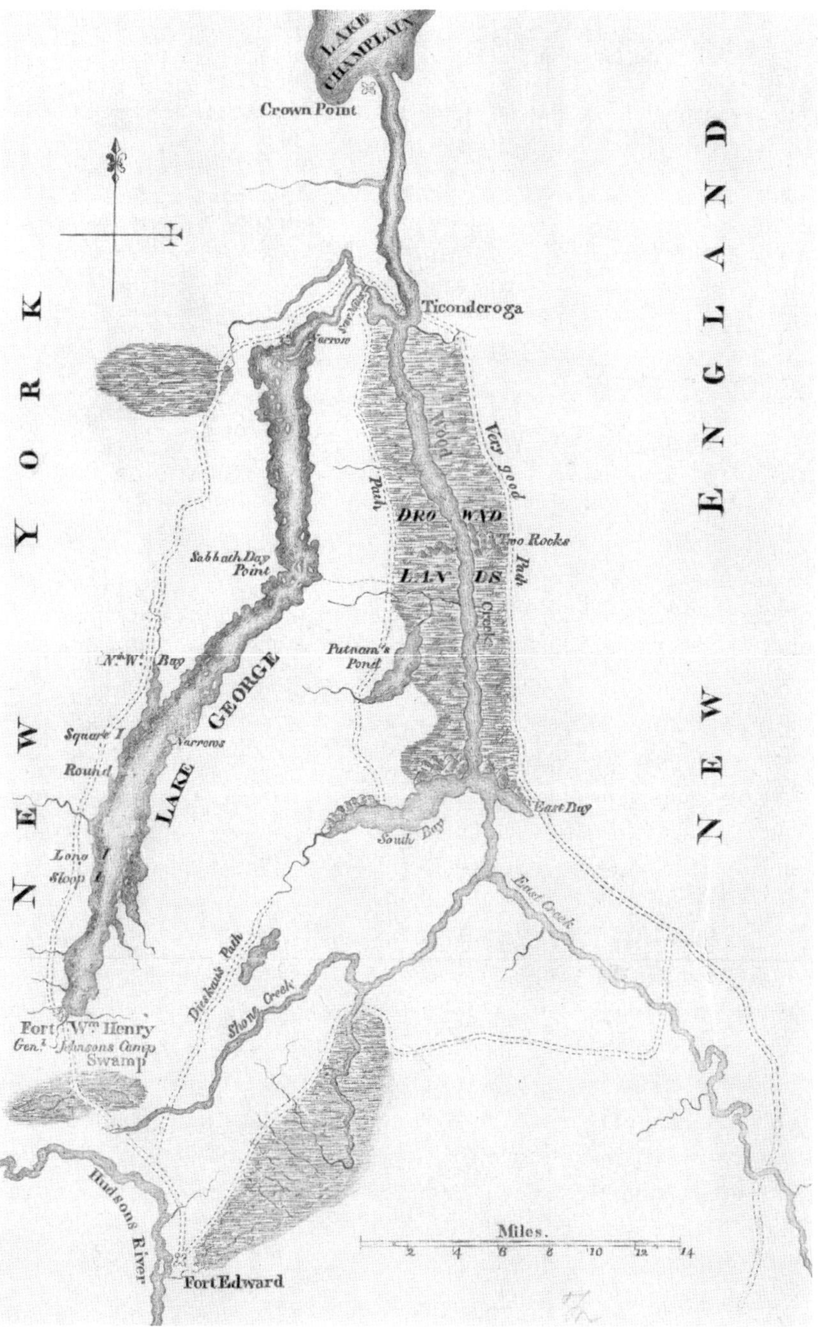

"A View of Lake George, Fort Ticonderoga, and the Vicinity." This would be the seat of war for Rogers' Rangers. *Courtesy of the Lionel Pincus and Princess Firyal Map Division, New York Public Library.*

importance; New France and the American colonies thus sent their forces to battle for its control.

The first group of Europeans to range in this area was a force commanded by Samuel de Champlain, namesake of the lake that was to become a battleground. His small French military force and their Native American allies fought the Iroquois at Carillon in 1609. Champlain and his allies won the day, but the French of New France had begun nearly a century of on-and-off warfare with the powerful Iroquois.[46]

After this punitive expedition, Champlain returned to his garrison house at Quebec. Except for missionaries, neither the French nor the Dutch, who were settling the Hudson Valley, nor the English who took over from them ventured into the area for many years to come. It was in King George's War at the end of the seventeenth century that the area took on the military importance it would keep through next century and after. And now the time had come when this valley was of paramount importance to both adversaries.[47]

Back in the Connecticut River Valley, tensions once again brought on the threat of war. In a meeting at Montreal, the Abenaki warned Phineas Stevens that they would not tolerate English settlement north of No. 4. They had heard that the English intended to build a road to and settle at Cowass (or Cohass, present-day Newbury) deep in their lands, and they stated multiple times that this could not be tolerated. The Province of New Hampshire took the Abenaki concerns seriously; however, when rumors came about that the French intended to build a fort there, it became strategically important to both sides.[48]

The deaths of two Abenaki men who departed from No. 4 on a hunting trip were the sparks that lit the powder keg. Just what happened to them is unclear, but the Abenaki of St. Francis accused the people of Charlestown of poisoning their alcohol. This hastened a decision of their own making, without French input, to go to war with New England once again. Ironically, though Charlestown seems to have been one of their chief antagonists, the area saw little warlike activity in the coming war, though there were clashes with Colonel Benjamin Bellows' garrison at Walpole and the kidnapping of the Johnson family near No. 4 in 1754.[49]

The fact that Charlestown did not see much involvement in the French and Indian War was a boon in several ways. In the first place, it meant that the Connecticut River Valley did not tie down British forces. Secondly, the Fort at No. 4 was an important base, staging area and supply depot during the war. Finally, it meant that the frontiersmen of the town, including

Phineas Stevens, who would die in service at Nova Scotia, were available for service on multiple fronts while other troops patrolled the area.

Though it was a few years before ranging reached its zenith, many knew from the beginning that experienced woodsmen were needed as scouts and skirmishers to fight in this harsh landscape. As the colonies of Great Britain raised provincial regiments to fight, each one had one or two companies of rangers in their order of battle. It was this kind of unit in the New Hampshire Regiment, and one man in particular, that would transform the British and American ways of war in the colonies.[50]

"HIS MAJESTY'S INDEPENDENT COMPANY OF RANGERS"

Robert Rogers was born on November 18, 1731, to Ulster Scot parents in Methuen, Massachusetts. At an early age, he and his family moved to New Hampshire, and when Rogers was only a teenager, he served in the militia during King George's War. By the time the next war rolled around, he was an imposing frontiersman standing over six feet tall. Nearly tried for counterfeiting, Rogers got a reprieve when war erupted with France and its Native American allies. He offered to recruit a force of soldiers to fight in the conflict, and in April 1755, the company was officially activated by the Province of New Hampshire as part of its provincial regiment.[51]

The only image of Robert Rogers from his lifetime, one that unfortunately does not convey the grit of the man. *Courtesy of the Miriam and Ira D. Wallach Division of Art, Prints and Photographs: Print Collection, New York Public Library.*

First serving in garrison duty, having missed the Battle of Lake George, Rogers soon became a man of importance. With much of the Mohawk force returning home after the battle to recover, the army needed a scouting force. He and his company of frontiersmen were nominated by Sir William Johnson to reconnoiter Lakes George and Champlain to Crown Point if possible.[52] Crown Point was known to the Franco-Canadians as the location of Fort-St.-Frederic, then their most southerly base in the Champlain Valley. A formidable fortification, it was also a base for French and Native American raiders in the area. If the British wanted to march up the great warpath to Montreal, this was a place that must be taken.[53]

Rogers and his men performed not one but several scouting forays into the wilderness, supplying his superiors with information and regaling comrades with their tales of derring-do. Having met with success, Rogers met with Governor William Shirley of Massachusetts, who was commanding all British forces in North America at the time. It was then, in the spring of 1756, when Shirley asked Rogers to form his own ranging

Portrait of Governor William Shirley of Massachusetts Bay by Thomas Hudson. He was one of the first to see promise in Rogers. *Courtesy of the National Portrait Gallery, Smithsonian Institution*

unit, the nucleus of which would be his company of New Hampshire men.[54]

This corps was independent of provincial ties, and though not termed *regulars*, they fell more directly under the control of the Crown and would thus be known as His Majesty's Independent Company of Rangers. Though technically only those in Robert Rogers' own company could claim to be so, anyone who served in the independent corps (and even other ranging companies from other provinces) has since come to be known under the famous title of "Rogers' Rangers."

One officer's commission from later in the war described the missions of the rangers, characterizing them as "men employed in obtaining intelligence of the strength situation and motions of the enemy as well as other service for which ranger or men acquainted with the woods only are fit." These men were to be the scouts or, in modern military parlance, the reconnaissance troops for both the provincials and British regulars.[55]

And it was just that kind of work that they dove into. The rangers helped provide escorts to supply convoys and scouted French positions with the intent of taking prisoners, like the later tactic of trench raiding in World War I. Many of the missions were performed in rough country several miles behind enemy lines, sometimes before the very gates of a French bastion. At first, the scouts involved were just Rogers and a few other men, but as the unit grew in importance, the forces involved in scouting missions increased as well.[56]

Squaring off against the rangers were a variety of forces, including newly arrived regulars from France, Canadian militia, colonial troops and New France's Native American allies. The latter two were the most like the rangers and therefore their most dangerous opponents. The colonial forces mostly consisted of the Compagnies Franches de la Marine, also called Troupes de la Marine. The colony of New France was administered to by the French navy rather than the army, hence the names of these companies. These troops were commanded by Canadian officers who reached their positions on merit, while the enlistees were mainly from France. Though they answered to the navy, it would have been harder to find men more suited to wilderness warfare. They bested their Anglo-American enemies many times.[57]

Then there were the Native Americans who elected to fight with France. These men proved to be masters of woodcraft, having gained these skills by living and hunting in the northern woods their entire lives. It was hard to beat "their ability to move silently through the woods, to follow trails,

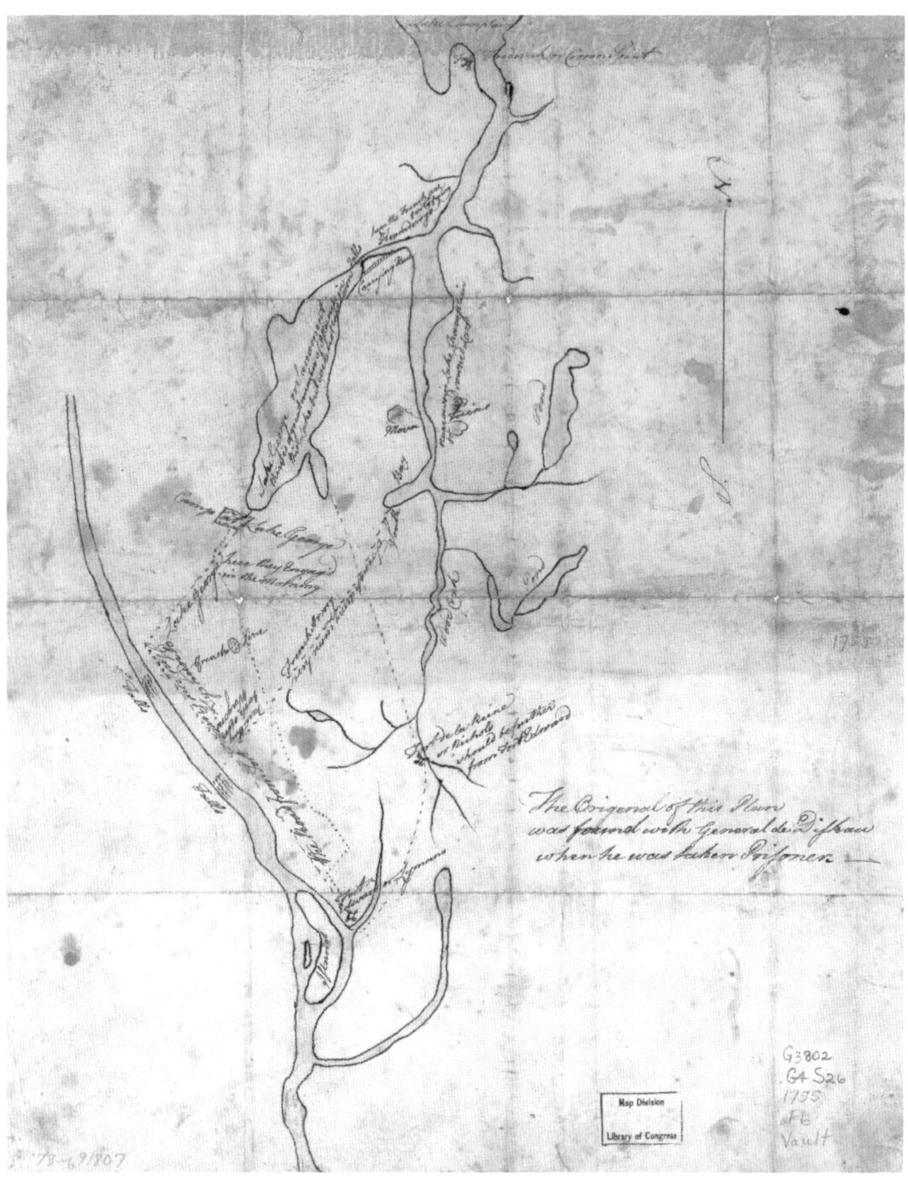

Above: Baron Dieskau's map of the area from Fort Edward to Crown Point. The detail on this map testifies to the intelligence gathering of Native American and irregular forces. *Courtesy of the Library of Congress, Geography and Map Division.*

Opposite: A 1755 Map of Crown Point's Defenses made by Robert Rogers for General William Johnson. *Courtesy of the Library of Congress, Geography and Map Division.*

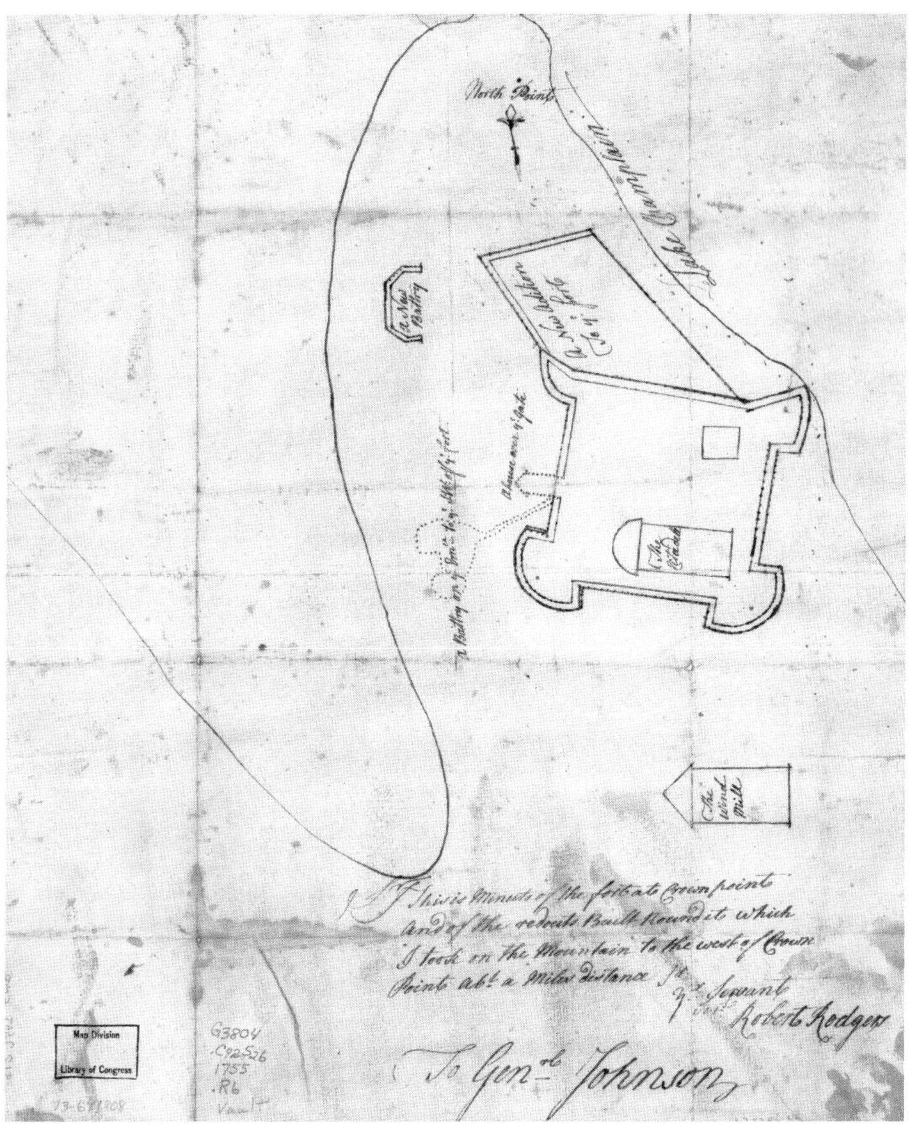

to survive using the materials of the forest for food, transportation, and shelter." Even frontiersmen such as Rogers' Rangers found it hard to compete against the Native Americans' literal home ground advantage.[58]

The military forces of New France were commanded by the Marquis de Vaudreuil, who served as governor of the colony, and the Marquis de Montcalm, who arrived with the regulars from France and took over the command of land forces following the capture of Baron Dieskau at the

Battle of Lake George. Vaudreuil believed in his predecessor Frontenac's raiding strategy, while Montcalm favored waging war in the European style when possible, such as at William Henry and Carillon. Though these strategies were vastly different, each proved an obstacle to the rangers fighting against them.[59]

The rangers also had to deal with enemy forces operating closer to their garrisons. Between 1755 and 1757, the French built a new fortress at Ticonderoga, the portage place between Lake Champlain and Lake George. Called Fort Carillon, this structure provided a dual threat, as it served as a base for French troops to operate south of Crown Point and meant mounting another siege if the British were to invade New France through this corridor.

The British had fortifications of their own, though. At the same time that the French were constructing Carillon, Fort Edward was constructed on the Hudson River; farther north, Fort William Henry was built on the south end of Lake George. For the first years of the war, Edward served as the base for British and provincial operations, while William Henry served as a more advanced operating base. The rangers were based primarily at Fort Edward on the Hudson on Rogers Island, but companies were stationed at William Henry, No. 4. and other areas of the theater.

La Barbue Creek

For eighteenth-century armies, the onset of winter usually meant going into winter quarters and a comparative lull settling over the front line. This was a time when the line infantry regiments stepped back, and raiders and irregular forces stepped forth. This was their hour and a time when they could be of the most use to their commanders. There were supply lines to be disrupted, scouts of positions to be made and prisoners to be captured and interrogated. Cometh the hour, cometh the man, and Rogers and his rangers set to work.

Rogers received orders to gather intelligence about the garrisons of Fort Carillon and Fort St. Frederic and to "harass the enemy in any way he saw fit." He took nearly one hundred rangers, mostly from his and his brother's companies, and snowshoes were prepared for the expedition. On January 15, 1757, the rangers left Fort Edward to proceed via Fort William Henry.

There, the expedition was joined by Captains Humphrey Hobbs' and Thomas Speakman's companies.[60]

Humphrey Hobbs had made a name for himself in the Connecticut River Valley during the last war. Thomas Speakman was a Boston native; his sister married merchant John Rowe, the owner of a shipment of tea to become famous in Boston almost two decades later. Both of these ranger captains were just as able as the Rogers brothers, and there was full trust in their abilities. The companies captained by the Rogers brothers were dressed in green buckskin, while Hobbs' and Speakman's companies wore gray coats and buckskin pants.[61]

Leaving on the evening of the seventeenth, the rangers marched several miles up Lake George before camping for the night. Rogers was forced to send over a dozen lame men back to William Henry. A couple of days later, Rogers' force had reached a point almost exactly in the middle of the two French fortifications, commonly called Five Mile Point near La Barbue Creek (present-day Five Mile Creek on the western side of Lake Champlain). There he prepared to ambush an incoming group of ten French supply sleighs being pulled across the lake by eighty horses and approximately thirty officers and men.[62]

"A View of Lake George." Its breathtaking scenery belies the carnage it witnessed. *Courtesy of the Miriam and Ira D. Wallach Division of Art, Prints and Photographs: Print Collection, New York Public Library.*

As two of the sleighs neared the rangers, they sprang from the lakeshore, capturing the two sleighs that had been forward of the rest of the group, though several of the enemy escaped on horseback. The rest of the group, seeing the fate of two of the sleighs, retreated to Fort Carillon. Rogers interrogated the seven prisoners taken and was able to learn more about the garrisons of the French fortresses. Their mission now accomplished and discovered, they had to return to British lines.[63]

Going against his own tactics and the advice of his fellow officers in a council of war, Rogers thought it best to retreat in the fastest way possible: the same way they had come. In this snow-covered theater of war, with so many scouting and raiding parties about, this was a risky decision. It was highly likely that French skirmishers or Native warbands had discovered Rogers' tracks and planned an ambush. Still, it was a risk he was willing to take. After drying their guns so that they might work after the morning rain, they set off at a quick pace.[64]

The men in the sleighs who had escaped to Carillon informed their superior officers of Rogers' presence. The French commander dispatched a force of one hundred men, containing regulars from the line infantry regiments, militia and Native American warriors. The French force located a ravine between two hills about three miles northwest of the fort and prepared an ambush in hope that Rogers might return that way. This they did, and as the rangers crested a side of the ravine, they must have felt a shiver of fear as they heard dozens of muskets cock. This was almost immediately followed by a volley of musketry and yells.[65]

Hit at almost point-blank range, the rangers' column shuddered under the onslaught. Rogers' hat was blown off by a round that grazed his head while Lieutenant Kennedy next to him fell dead, along with about a dozen others. Rogers, despite his wound, ordered his men to get back to the other side of the ravine. A French officer led a charge by Ottawa warriors to try to engage the rangers in hand-to-hand combat. Several rangers fell beneath the assault, but worse was prevented by John Stark and Ensign Jonathan Brewer rallying their men on their side of the ravine and beating back the French and Ottawa with their fire.[66]

The French called to Rogers to surrender, but this he promptly refused. A standoff ensued until nightfall, when, after beating off one more assault by the Ottawa seeking scalps, Rogers ordered a retreat. Toward the end of the engagement, he received a serious wound in the wrist. The dead, those near it and many of the wounded left behind were scalped. One of those who was killed after the battle was Captain Speakman. Rogers and fifty-three others made it back to British lines after Stark had been sent ahead to get sleighs for the wounded. At least one of the prisoners taken earlier had been killed per Rogers' orders, so none would escape to give their location away.[67]

General John Campbell, Fourth Earl of Loudoun, the British commander who commissioned Noah Porter as a ranger officer. *Courtesy of the Miriam and Ira D. Wallach Division of Art, Prints and Photographs: Print Collection, New York Public Library.*

The rangers' first large skirmish came to be known as the Battle of La Barbue Creek, or the First Battle on Snowshoes. Rogers' men were mauled, but they still had proved their worth in the winter wilderness. One of the rangers killed in the engagement was Andrew Gardiner, whom Burt Garfield Loescher states was from Charlestown. Gardiner was a cadet in Rogers' own company, seeking to attain the rank of ensign in the corps. He was likely killed in the opening volley from the French; his dreams of a commission in the rangers ended with death in the snowy wilderness.[68]

The rangers suffered losses during this battle and continued to lose men to fatigue and illness. Sanctioned by his superiors, Rogers was to launch a recruiting campaign to get more men to join the corps. This was mostly to be managed by his brother while he recovered from the wound to his wrist. His rangers had done well gathering intelligence and conducting small raids, even if they had just received a bloody nose from the French and their allies, and Rogers continued to enjoy the confidence of his commanders like Lord Loudoun.

Adding to the Corps

Recruiting lieutenants and sergeants were sent across New England, mainly reporting to Captain Richard Rogers, brother of Robert, who was performing administrative duties in Boston. Noah Porter from the Fort at No. 4 was typical of the kind of New England frontiersman who joined the rangers. He was born on May 6, 1734, in Northfield, Massachusetts, to frontiersman and former ranger James Porter and his wife, Experience Wright. Experience's father was Benjamin, the renowned "Indian fighter" of earlier wars.[69]

According to local lore,

> *The Porter brothers, James, William, and Noah, were bold and dauntless men, and inspired, in the minds of the Indians such fear that they were left unmolested by their attacks. At the time Joseph Willard and family were taken prisoners by them, they took the greatest precaution to keep the knowledge of their movements from the Porters, who had the reputation of never missing their aim, and traditions still linger of their intrepidity and daring. They did not hesitate to attack the fiercest beasts, and it is not known that they were ever worsted in any encounter.*
>
> *It is a tradition that that they were out one time on a hunting expedition and had encamped for the night. As it began to grow dark, they heard what they at first took to be the hooting of an owl, which was soon answered by a similar hoot, in another direction. They then heard the same in other directions; and their quick ears soon discovered that the sounds were signals given by a company of Indians, who had surrounded them, and were gradually centering in towards the encampment. They listened and found that the Indians very much exceeded them in number, and taking advantage of the signals, they very carefully threaded their way out between their enemies and escaped. In order to avoid the possibility of pursuit by dogs, in case their enemies might have any, they made their way to a brook, the stream of which they followed down to a considerable difference, so that the scent of their footsteps could not be traced.*[70]

These were exactly the kinds of tactics used by the rangers under Rogers.

When some of the settlers from No. 4. attempted to settle land across the Connecticut River, Noah Porter was among them. As historian Frederick Richardson wrote, "They came with no money and with whatever they had on their backs or could carry on their canoes." They were forced to stop their efforts when the war broke out and for the most part remained at the fort throughout the conflict.[71]

Porter enlisted as a private in Rogers' own company on May 25, 1757. It is sometimes said that the Noah Porter of Farmington, Connecticut, was

Sabbath Day Point on Lake George. *Courtesy of the Miriam and Ira D. Wallach Division of Art, Prints and Photographs: Print Collection, New York Public Library.*

the one who served in Rogers' Rangers, though he actually served with Connecticut provincial troops at the same time as this Noah Porter was an enlisted man in the rangers, and therefore he could not have been in Rogers' own company at the same time.[72]

After enlisting, he would have made his way to Fort Edward on the Hudson River Valley, probably a journey of a couple days. As a recruit, he was trained by his sergeant and First Lieutenant John McCurdy, who had replaced John Stark after the latter assumed command of the late Captain Speakman's company. He received two shillings and six pence a day, with a subtraction of ten dollars in the beginning due to bounty money received. This would convert roughly to about sixteen U.S. dollars a day in the America of the 2020s and for that time was the same daily rate of pay as a skilled tradesman in England, a fit compensation for paying a man with woodsman's skills.[73]

It should be noted that around this time, two companies of rangers were raised from New Hampshire under Captains Shepherd and Titcomb. These were at times subordinated to Robert Rogers but were not technically part of Rogers' Rangers, as His Majesty's Independent Company of American Rangers became known. The latter was paid for by the British government, while the two New Hampshire companies were paid for by their provincial government.

It is not known whether Porter made it to Rogers' company in time to participate in the failed expedition to reduce the fortress of Louisbourg in Nova Scotia. The rangers left the Albany area for New York Harbor in early May and sailed for Halifax on June 18, and with him having just joined, it seems more likely that he did not take part. He would not have missed much, as the expedition was a failure; the French navy had reinforced the garrison, making an assault impractical. Rogers' Rangers spent the better part of their time rounding up deserters, cutting hay (which they detested) and getting into fights with Gorham's Rangers, a Nova Scotia–based British unit.

ROGERS' RULES

The following are Rogers' rules for the ranging service as he set them down in his journals postwar. He included them in his discussions of events in 1757, and that is likely when he set them down at the request of Lord Loudoun. If the reader is not interested in eighteenth-century ranger tactics, he may skip over them; however, the author recommends reading them for insight into how these men worked and fought in the wilderness in wartime.[74]

> *All Rangers are to be subject to the rules and articles of war; to appear at roll-call every evening on their own parade, equipped, each with sixty rounds of powder and ball, and a hatchet, at which time an officer from each company is to inspect the same, to see they are in order, so as to be ready for any emergency at a minute's warning; and before they are dismissed the necessary guards are to be draughted, and scouts for the next day appointed.*
>
> *Whenever you are ordered out to the enemies forts or frontiers for discoveries, if your number be small, march in a single file, keeping at such a distance from each other as to prevent one shot from killing two men, sending one man, or more, forward, and the like on each side, at the distance of twenty yards from the main body, if the ground you march over will admit of it, to give the signal to the officer of the approach of an enemy, and of their number, &c.*

If you march over marshes or soft ground, change your position, and march abreast of each other, to prevent the enemy from tracking you, (as they would do if you marched in a single file) till you get over such ground, and then resume your former order, and march till it is quite dark before you encamp, which do, if possible, on a piece of ground that may afford your centries the advantage of seeing or hearing the enemy at some considerable distance, keeping one half of your party awake alternately through the night.

Some time before you come to the place you would reconnoitre, make a stand, and send one or two men, in whom you can confide, to look out the best ground for making your observations.

If you have the good fortune to take any prisoners, keep them separate, till they are examined, and in your return take a different rout from that in which you went out, that you may the better discover any party in your rear, and have an opportunity, if their strength be superior to yours, to alter your course, or disperse, as circumstances may require.

If you march in a large body of three or four hundred, with a design to attack the enemy, divide your party into three columns, each headed by a proper officer, and let these columns march in single files, the columns to the right and left keeping at twenty yards distance or more from that of the center, if the ground will admit, and let proper guards be kept in the front and rear, and suitable flanking parties at a due distance as before directed, with orders to halt on all eminences, to take a view of the surrounding ground, to prevent your being ambuscaded, and to notify the approach or retreat of an enemy, that proper dispositions may be made for attacking, defending, &c. And if the enemy approach in your front on level ground, form a front of your three columns or main body with the advanced guard, keeping out your flanking parties, as if you were marching under the command of trusty officers, to prevent the enemy from pressing hard on either of your wings, or surrounding you, which is the usual method of the savages, if their number will admit of it, and be careful likewise to support and strengthen your rear-guard.

If you are obliged to receive the enemy's fire, fall, or squat down, till it is over, then rise and discharge at them. If their main body is equal to yours, extend yourselves occasionally, but if superior, be careful to support and strengthen your flanking parties, to make them equal with theirs, that if possible you may repulse them to their main body, in which case push upon them with the greatest resolution, with equal force in each flank and in the center, observing to keep at a due distance from each other, and advance from tree to tree, with one half of the party before the other ten or twelve yards. If the enemy push upon you, let your front fire and fall down, and then let your rear advance thro' them and do the like, by which time those who before were in front will be ready to discharge again, and repeat the same alternately, as occasion shall require; by this means you will keep such a constant fire, that the enemy will not be able easily to break your order, or gain your ground.

If you oblige the enemy to retreat, be careful, in your pursuit of them, to keep out your flanking parties, and prevent them from gaining eminences, or rising grounds, in which case they would perhaps be able to rally and repulse you in their turn.

If you are obliged to retreat, let the front of your whole party fire and fall back, till the rear hath done the same, making for the best ground you can; by this means you will oblige the enemy to pursue you, if they do it at all, in the face of a constant fire.

If the enemy is so superior that you are in danger of being surrounded by them, let the whole body disperse, and every one take a different road to the place of rendezvous appointed that evening, which must every morning be altered and fixed for the evening ensuing, in order to bring the whole party, or as many of them as possible, together, after any separation that may happen in the day; but if you should happen to be actually surrounded, form yourselves into a square, or if in the woods, a circle is best, and if possible, make a stand till the darkness of the night favours your escape.

If your rear is attacked, the main body and flankers must face about to the right or left, as occasion shall require, and form themselves to oppose the enemy, as before directed; and the same method must be observed, if attacked in either of your flanks, by which means you will always make a rear of one of your flank-guards.

If you determine to rally after a retreat, in order to make a fresh stand against the enemy, by all means endeavour to do it on the most rising ground you can come at, which will give you greatly the advantage in point of situation, and enable you to repulse superior numbers.

In general, when pushed upon by the enemy, reserve your fire till they approach very near, which will then put them into the greater surprize and consternation, and give you an opportunity of rushing upon them with your hatchets and cutlasses to the better advantage.

When you encamp at night, fix your centries in such a manner as not to be relieved from the main body till morning, profound secrecy and silence being often of the last importance in these cases. Each centry, therefore, should consist of six men, two of whom must be constantly alert, and when relieved by their fellows, it should be done without noise; and in case those on duty see or hear any thing, which alarms them, they are not to speak, but one of them is silently to retreat, and acquaint the commanding officer thereof, that proper dispositions may be made; and all occasional centries should be fixed in like manner.

At the first dawn of day, awake your whole detachment; that being the time when the savages chuse to fall upon their enemies, you should by all means be in readiness to receive them.

If the enemy should be discovered by your detachments in the morning, and their numbers are superior to yours, and a victory doubtful, you should not attack them till the evening, as then they will not know your numbers, and if you are repulsed, your retreat will be favored in the darkness of the night.

Before you leave your encampment, send out small parties to scout round it, to see if there be any appearance or track of an enemy that might have been near you during the night.

When you stop for refreshment, chuse some spring or rivulet if you can, and dispose your party so as not to be surprised, posting proper guards and centries at a due distance, and let a small party waylay the path you came in, lest the enemy should be pursuing.

If, in your return, you have to cross rivers, avoid the usual fords as much as possible, lest the enemy should have discovered, and be there expecting you.

If you have to pass by lakes, keep at some distance from the edge of the water, lest, in case of ambuscade, or an attack from the enemy, when in that situation, your retreat should be cut off.

If the enemy pursue your rear, take a circle till you come to your own tracks, and there form an ambush to receive them, and give them the first fire.

When you return from a scout, and come near our forts, avoid the usual roads, and avenues thereto, lest the enemy should have headed you, and lay in ambush to receive you, when almost exhausted with fatigues.

When you pursue any party that has been near our forts or encampments, follow not directly in their tracks, lest you should be discovered by their rear-guards, who, at such a time, would be most alert; but endeavour, by a different route, to head and meet them in some narrow pass, or lay in ambush to receive them when and where they least expect it.

If you are to embark in canoes, battoes, or otherwise, by water, chuse the evening for the time of your embarkation, as you will then have the whole night before you, to pass undiscovered by any parties of the enemy, on hills, or other places, which command a prospect of the lake or river you are upon.

In padling or rowing, give orders that the boat or canoe the next sternmost, wait for her, and the third for the second, and the fourth for the third, and so on, to prevent separation, and that you may be ready to assist each other on any emergency.

Appoint one man in each boat to look out for fires, on the adjacent shores, from the numbers and size of which you may form some judgement of the number that kindled them, and whether you are able to attack them or not.

If you find the enemy encamped near the banks of a river, or lake, which you imagine they will attempt to cross for their security upon being attacked, leave a detachment of your party on the opposite shore to receive them, while with the remainder, you surprize them, having them between you and the lake or river.

If you cannot satisfy yourself to the enemy's number and strength, from their fire, &c. conceal your boats at some distance, and ascertain

> *their number by a reconnoitering party, when they embark, or march, in the morning, marking the course they steer &c. when you may pursue, ambush, and attack them, or let them pass, as prudence shall direct you. In general, however, that you may not be discovered by the enemy on the lakes and rivers at a great distance, it is safest to lay by, with your boats and party concealed all day, without noise or shew, and to pursue your intended route by night; and whether you go by land or water, give out parole and countersigns, in order to know one another in the dark, and likewise appoint a station for every man to repair to, in case of any accident that may separate you.*

LIFE IN THE RANGER SERVICE

The rangers were a light, mobile reconnaissance force known for their ability to move through the wilderness. As such, there was a limit to what supplies they could take with them. Provisions, weapons and blankets were about all they could carry. Food supplies could dictate a mission's duration and targets; when it ran low, the men would try to hunt game and, failing all else, ate tree bark and anything they could stomach.[75]

Being in enemy territory, it was sometimes too dangerous to light a fire, and the men had to bundle up as best they could in an area that can experience temperatures as low as forty degrees below zero. The men could brace themselves from the elements by making pine bough shelters and bundling up in their blankets until they had become like "human cocoons." When a fire could be lit, the men slept around it in a circle with their feet facing the fire so that everyone had a chance of getting some heat.[76]

Vermont historian Benjamin Hall provides a wonderful description of camping while on a scout:

> *Were it summer, the ground sufficed for a bed, the clear sky or the out-spreading branches of some giant oak for a canopy. Were it winter, at the close of a weary march, performed on snow-shoes, a few gathered twigs pointed the couch made hard by necessity, and a rude hut served as a shelter from the misery of the weather. Were the night very dark and cold, and no fear of discovery entertained, gathering around the blazing brush heap, they enjoyed a kind of satisfaction at that towering of its bright, forked*

> *flame, relieved by the dark background of the black forest; or encircling it in slumber, dreamed that there* [sic] *heads were in Greenland, and their feet in Vesuvius.*[77]

As stated earlier, compared to the provincial troops and especially the British regulars, the rangers were well paid. There was also the chance of bounty money from enemy prisoners or scalps taken and a bounty to purchase clothes or a uniform, weapons and other necessaries. And, as Ranger historian Gary Zaboly stated, "by signing up he would help quicken the inevitable fall of New France, which would both end the Indian raids on the frontier towns and open up the vast Abenaki hunting grounds to settlement, including sizeable land grants for war veterans."[78]

Through the early years of the war, the rangers wore what they had as civilian woodsmen and frontiersmen, mostly short cut clothes of a plain color, with elements of borrowed Native American styles and garments. In the winter of 1758, Rogers ordered green uniforms with white buttons for his men, with the officers' uniforms having "silver lacing and cord or braid." Aside from the greatcoats, most of the other parts of the uniforms were made of a thinner wool, which, combined with the coat, could help prepare Rangers for year-round temperatures.[79] The hats they wore were "balmoral scotch bonnets," no doubt a nod to the heritage of Rogers and many of his men, as well as Lords Loudoun and Abercrombie.[80]

Rangers typically carried their food provisions in knapsacks hung over the shoulder. Loescher stated that "provisions consisted of two weeks supply of dried beef, sugar, rice, and dried peas and cornmeal. In their wooden canteens each ranger carried rum." Besides satiating the rangers' desire for spirits, the alcoholic beverage was always a safe bet in an era before the science of water treatment could make most streams potable.[81]

The men recruited into the rangers, primarily men experienced in living in the wilderness, were encouraged to bring their own equipment and guns. Historian Gary Zaboly wrote that the governor of New Hampshire cautioned recruits to "find themselves arms…as the King's Arms are very heavy." As such, though muskets were in use, the rangers were mostly using rifles by early 1758, before the start of the Fort Carillon campaign. Their tactics demanded skirmishing and accuracy, something that the rifle was much better equipped for.[82]

Muskets of the period have become legendary for their inaccuracy. It is not so much that a musket such as the famous "Brown Bess" was a poor weapon, but it lacked rifling, meaning it had a smooth bore. Musket balls were not made to fit the width of the barrel (lest they be too big and get stuck or clog it) but were slightly smaller. Thus, when the ball was fired, it would move from side to side down the barrel in what is called windage. This

To Range the Woods by SP4 Manuel B. Ablaza, U.S. Army. Note the difference in uniforms between the rangers and the British regular. *Courtesy of the U.S. Army Center for Military History, Army Artist Team XXII.*

unpredictable movement means that when the ball leaves the barrel, it will most likely have a slight directional attitude other than straight, and there was no telling what that would be!

For this reason, musket-armed troops were often formed into line of battle, having rows of men discharge their weapons either independently or in a volley at the same target, assuring that some hits would be registered. Hoping to hit a target with a musket at anything but close range is a gamble, and having soldiers fire in line was a way of making that gamble more likely to pay off.

As many men were professional hunters, it comes as no surprise that many of them were good shots. One officer of the Twenty-Seventh Regiment of Foot described their accuracy and said that even garrisoned they formed scouting and hunting parties to keep their skills sharp.[83] It was not just eye that made these men good shots though—it was also their rifles, which differ from muskets in having a rifled barrel, spinning the ball like the modern football player, giving it a straighter and, in this case, much deadlier course. Their experience as hunters also allowed them to perform better in battle, as after firing they might quickly reload by spitting another ball down the barrel, cutting down on the usual thirty-second reload time.[84]

Hand-to-hand combat was an important part of the rangers' tactics and a near certainty in an enemy engagement. Rogers let his men fire only when the enemy were close, and once they had done so, they charged the enemy to fight in close quarters with tomahawks and scalping knives. In the wintertime, this also meant one fighter trying to break the other's snowshoes, as movement was incredibly difficult in the deep drifts encountered. Broken snowshoes meant that a combatant was both at an immediate disadvantage and would also have trouble retreating later.[85]

Being reconnaissance troops, the rangers participated in intense, small-scale skirmishes and ambushes more often than large set-piece battles. Rogers' men were usually involved in setting ambushes and trying not to walk into French ones. If the latter did occur, the rangers attempted to withdraw while inflicting as many casualties as possible. This usually meant keeping up a steady fire, as hand-to-hand combat against a larger force can be deadly. Sometimes withdrawing meant slipping directly through the enemy's lines, as the Porter brothers did once while on a hunting trip.[86]

Siege and Massacre at Fort William Henry

In the meantime, the French had not been idle. Led by Montcalm, the French sacked Oswego and captured Fort William Henry. The latter victory was tainted by the following massacre of the British and provincial prisoners at the hands of Montcalm's Native American allies, an event made famous in James Fenimore Cooper's novel *The Last of the Mohicans*. The French then retreated up the Champlain Valley, though not before ruining Fort William Henry for any immediate military use.

The horrors of modern war are known to those of us who live in the twenty-first century, but the "honors of war" were much more respected in the 1750s. A unit of soldiers then was not expected to fight until the last man like the battles of the Second World War. Men fought, and there would be killed or wounded, but if they surrendered, they could hope for humane treatment; they might be led away as prisoners or, as at William Henry, paroled on agreement they would not participate in the campaign for a certain period. That such an agreement was shattered by a massacre at the hands of Montcalm's allies only added to the shock.

The rangers present at William Henry were those of Captain Richard Rogers' company. Rogers, the younger brother of Robert, had died at the fort the previous June of smallpox, and his company was being led by Lieutenant Noah Johnson. When the garrison surrendered, this company surrendered as well. Some were taken by the Native Americans, and although one was reportedly tortured to death, others were fortunate enough to be taken prisoner and some exchanged. Even the corpses of those who died of smallpox over the summer were not safe. According to his brother, the body of the late Richard Rogers was exhumed and scalped. The surviving company was disbanded per the terms of the capitulation agreement with the French. The gauntlet had been thrown down.[87]

This disaster in the northwest frontier hastened the return of the rangers from Nova Scotia. Returning to Albany by mid-September, they then began a course of instruction in ranging for British regulars. This program was a must for any soldier who wanted a commission with the British regulars as well. All the while, Rogers continued to send out scouting and hunting parties. It was during this time that General Lord Howe went on a scout with Rogers.[88]

George Augustus, Third Viscount Howe, was a great-nephew of King George I and brother to Admiral Richard Howe, First Earl Howe, and General William Howe, both of whom would play significant roles in the

American and French Revolutionary Wars. George Augustus inherited the Earldom of Howe upon the death of his father in 1735 and entered the British army in 1745 as an ensign in the First Regiment of Foot Guards. He quickly rose through the ranks following the War of Austrian Succession and by 1757 had been sent to America as colonel of the Royal American Regiment, followed soon after by command of the Fifty-Fifth Regiment of Foot. Lord Howe appreciated Rogers' ability in wilderness warfare and applied many of the lessons to the training of his own unit. His leadership and charisma endeared him not only to his fellow soldiers but also to civilians in both the American colonies and Great Britain.[89]

General George Augustus, Lord Viscount Howe, whose death would change the course of the 1758 campaign and American history. *Courtesy of the Miriam and Ira D. Wallach Division of Art, Prints and Photographs: Print Collection, New York Public Library.*

Mutiny

The patrols and hunting expeditions notwithstanding, the remainder of 1757 mostly held few opportunities for action for Rogers' Rangers. One of the many lessons taught by history is that idleness in soldiers bodes ill for all involved. The independent nature of the rangers and their fondness of their rum allowance (and more so) only compounded this problem. Rogers responded to disciplinary problems by discharging offending rangers, but this was no longer feasible. He was forced to turn to the regular military practice of flogging.[90]

Flogging was a punishment that involved whipping a soldier across his back with a cat-o'-nine-tails, which, as the name implies, involved multiple lengths of rope stemming from one handle. The brutal practice has since become infamously linked with the British Royal Navy, but the first recorded ranger to be punished was Samuel Leech, who refused to go on a scout until he had his rum allowance. The final straw came with the imprisonment of Samuel Boyd and Henry Dawson, igniting what came to be known as the "whipping post mutiny."[91]

Evidently, the rangers had had enough, because on the night of December 6, 1757, a mob of rangers began to form out in the street between huts. Some had said that if the flogging were to continue, there would "be no more rangers."[92] Dissenters, apparently led by Privates Abraham Parrot and Noah Porter of Rogers' own company, marched to the whipping post. There, ranger Joshua Atwood used an axe to fell the post, an act cheered on by the rangers nearby.[93]

They then made their way to the guardhouse where Boyd and Dawson were kept and demanded their release. When the guards refused, they attempted to dismantle the roof and force their way in, and it was at this point that Captain Shepherd arrived and ordered the rangers to disperse. In reply, one of the rangers pointed a gun at the officer and told him to stay out of the affair. Two of Stark's rangers seized the man, and Shepherd disarmed him. It was then that Captain Bulkeley appeared and again told the rangers to disperse. Bulkeley was apparently more respected than Shepherd, as the men complied, while six of the instigators were placed under arrest as mutineers.[94]

The men were held in the custody of Lieutenant Colonel Haviland of the Twenty-Seventh (Inniskilling) Regiment of Foot while a court of inquiry was held with Rogers as the president. Captain Shepherd stated he was not sure which ranger pointed a firearm at him, an odd thing to either miss or forget considering the circumstances. Officers and enlisted alike professed that they were ignorant as to who was involved in the mutiny. The identity of the ranger who threatened Captain Shepherd with a gun was said to be either Parrott or Porter, but eventually the main part of suspicion fell on Parrott, as several rangers said the gun confiscated was his.[95]

Though Parrott was now the ranger with the most to lose, all the rangers were still in the frying pan. Sergeant Moore of Rogers' company said that on the day of the mutiny, he heard Porter say "in a poking way he thought the whipping post would not last long," a remark that, put together with his involvement in the events of that evening, certainly seemed like mutinous behavior.[96]

Though somewhat inconclusive, the minutes of the court of inquiry were forwarded to General Abercrombie by Colonel Haviland. The British officer made strong recommendations for a general court martial, and if a conviction was achieved, the mutineers should be "severely punished."

Rogers hoped that the matter could be settled, as he feared his men would desert otherwise. Haviland replied with an offer to hang anyone who tried that "as an example." General Abercrombie in turn passed the decision onto Lord Loudoun.[97]

This incident shows just what kind citizen soldiers Rogers' Rangers were. These men were tough fighters who knew their craft well, but if an officer had tried to get them to perform all the fancy steps of the regulars as on the parade ground, he would have been disappointed. Though the rangers of the U.S. Army of today claim descent from Rogers' and other units—and in skill sets this can be quite true—they were a world apart when it comes to discipline.[98]

Rogers was sent on a scout by Haviland, likely to get the former out of the latter's way. But upon his return, Rogers met with Lord Loudoun, who was not only happy to gloss over the mutiny incident but also asked Rogers to form more companies of rangers for the corps, with Loudoun eventually approving five. In addition, Thomas Gage of the Forty-Fourth Regiment of Foot would bear the cost of forming a light regiment, a hybrid between the regulars and the rangers, that became the Eightieth Regiment of Foot.[99]

Shockingly, one of the benefactors of this development was mutineer Noah Porter. Having gained his release, Rogers promoted and recommended Porter as the first lieutenant of Moses Brewer's new company, which was mainly composed of Mohegan Indians, being commissioned by Lord Loudoun on January 14, 1758. Rogers must have thought highly of Porter to change a man from mutineer to officer nearly overnight. The other rangers involved in the "whipping post mutiny" were either demoted or discharged.[100]

7

THE FRENCH AND INDIAN WAR, 1758-63

Britain Triumphant

Mohegan Rangers

Unlike their French enemies, the Anglo-American forces relied less on Native American auxiliaries. As historian Eliot Cohen put it, "The Indians understood that the English sought to settle, whereas the French were content to trade, dominate, and convert." With the exceptions of the Mohawk, Mohegan and Stockbridge Mohican warriors who served in companies inside and outside of Rogers' Rangers, the Native American tribes in this theater of the war maintained a kind of neutrality policy and waited to see which European empire would achieve victory.[101]

Looking back on this unit through a more modern lens, a question arises: Why were these warriors led by White officers? This arrangement does not seem to be a racial one but one based on personal stake. This war was, at its heart, between two European kings and their nations on ground that just happened to be in North America. If the British had merely wanted the Mohicans and Mohegans to fight, they might have just asked and/or paid them to. But as the Rangers and their British superiors had their own plans for what they wanted done and where, it made sense to have their own officers in charge of these Native American warriors to carry these plans out. That is why in addition to being in units from their tribe, warriors were in units that could be termed auxiliary to the British.

The Mohegans are a tribe often confused with the more northerly located Mohicans (also called Mahicans). The Mohegan people have historically lived in central Connecticut and parts of Rhode Island and Massachusetts; there are some who continue to reside in Connecticut to this day. Having escaped the fate of the Pequot people during the infamous Pequot War, they had since then mostly remained on good terms with the English, at least as good as a dwindling Indigenous people could manage.

As Mohican and Mohegan were interchangeable even in the mid-eighteenth century, it is hard to tell just who was serving with the British or provincial forces. The service of Mohicans from Stockbridge, Massachusetts, is well documented. As far as the Mohegans of Brewer's Company, the historical waters have become muddied. They are referred to as Mohicans so often it is hard to separate the two, but given Brewer's background of coming from south-central Massachusetts, it seems most likely that his company did contain actual Mohegan warriors and not their northern neighbors.

The leader of this unit, Captain Moses Brewer, was born in Framingham, Massachusetts, but eventually moved to nearby Sherborn and then Sudbury. He served in Nova Scotia in 1757 and was then recommended by Rogers for the captaincy of the Mohegan company. He served through 1759 and apparently did not live long after the war, dying in the 1760s. His most conspicuous services were in the campaigns against Forts Carillon and St. Frederic in 1759.[102]

Two second lieutenants also served with the company, the first being Mohegan warrior Joseph Duquipe. He served through the year and then again in 1760, going with Rogers on his expedition to Detroit as the commander of the Mohegan detachment. The other second lieutenant was Joseph Johnson, another Mohegan warrior who also served through 1758. Unfortunately, the names of noncommissioned officers (or Mohegan equivalent) and warriors are still unknown to the author currently.[103]

The only other known ranger listed as serving with Brewer's Company through 1758 is the company clerk, Lawrence Ekins of Hanover, Massachusetts. He was listed as a deserter in the *Boston Evening Post* in the summer of 1759, having apparently absconded with the company strongbox. Anyone with information about his whereabouts was to report to the apparent wife of Captain Brewer in Sudbury. Nothing more being said about the man, he seems to have made his getaway.[104]

The Mohegan warriors were not issued uniforms as both a cost-saving measure and because it was thought that their own style of dress and war paint were more formidable on the battlefield. No man of European descent had ever been recorded as saying that Native Americans did not understand camouflage. Porter and the other officers likely wore the style of officer's uniform mentioned earlier or their own hunting and woodsmen's clothing. All officers had "compasses in the large end of their powder horns," for navigating the woods and waterways.[105]

Rogers Rock

Porter was fortunate to have left Rogers' company when he did, as it just might have saved his life. Rogers had been developing a plan to raid French supply sleighs with four hundred rangers and then use them to capture Fort Carillon in a coup de main, pretending to be the French sleigh party returning from their supply run. Lord Loudoun seemed to consider the plan, but it had since been put to the side, as well as being talked about too publicly for Rogers' liking.

To get Rogers out of his way while he sought to determine the fate of the mutineers, and out of a general dislike of the man, Colonel Haviland ordered him to conduct the raid. But Rogers was allocated a force of fewer than two hundred rangers, a force reduction of over 50 percent. Still, Rogers was an officer in the king's service and he had orders to follow. The force departed from Fort Edward on March 10, 1758.[106]

With a force of picked men from the rangers and some officers and men from the regulars, they made their way up Lake George via the ruins of Fort William Henry. His force was not the only one in the area, as a force of French colonial troops, Iroquois and Nipissing warriors was also garrisoned at their fort, purportedly acting on the visions of a shaman from the night they arrived at Carillon. When a party of Native American warriors came across Rogers' trail near Bald Mountain on the western shore of Lake George, they alerted this force, which immediately marched.

A small group of Native American warriors rushed out to find the rangers, while a larger force commanded by Levrault de Langis, arguably Rogers' French counterpart, followed behind them.[107]

Seeing the smaller party from Fort Carillon arriving first, Rogers deployed his men to trap the warriors in a depression in the ground that formed a kind of kill zone. The plan worked, with the force routed on the rangers' first volley. Rogers' force pursued the survivors and began scalping the dead, without having reloaded, as his own "rules of ranging" advocated, and had tomahawks and knives at the ready. They ran down their quarry straight into Langis' force, which, in a burst of thunder, smoke and flame, produced an ambush volley of their own.[108]

Rogers lost about a third of his force to this volley, approximately fifty men killed or wounded, with the survivors immediately set upon by knife and tomahawk. The right flank of Rogers' force had been shattered, and it seemed likely that the rest would soon follow. Rogers remained calm and rallied his men and turned the rout into a fighting withdrawal up a nearby slope. Amid the din of battle were heard the cries of anguish from the Native Americans who found the bodies of those killed by the rangers first, and this rage was channeled into a butchering of the wounded rangers.[109]

Rogers' men were still fighting as a unit, but facing a force double the size of their own they soon had over one hundred casualties. Retreating further up the hill, the rangers then played for time until nightfall, when those able could scatter and make their escape. Just exactly how they managed to do this without being massacred is not clear, but a couple of hours later they had made it to the shore of Lake George.[110]

The escape of Rogers and the other survivors gave birth to a legend that has ingrained itself in geography. Rogers reportedly made it down to the lake by sliding down Bald Mountain's rock face, a height of some 700 feet. This is rather unlikely, but the legend has survived longer than the facts have. What was formerly called Bald Mountain came to be known as Rogers Rock, and the steep face that he was supposed to have slid down is called Rogers Slide.[111]

Rogers returned to British lines with about fifty men; while there were some rangers taken prisoner, the great majority had been killed in the action or executed after or left to the elements which were deadly enough. That Rogers' force was able to hit "over two dozen Indians" during the action is a testament to the accuracy of his men's shooting. A fleet-of-foot Native American warrior experienced in woodland warfare is hard to hit, and so many killed or wounded was indeed a grievous loss to them. Each warrior lost or crippled would be felt in hunting or gathering a harvest among an already depopulated people.[112]

Rogers had suffered another catastrophic defeat at the hand of the French and their Native American allies, but he and his unit had managed to survive, even if it was just barely so. The companies could be rebuilt, and new officers could be found for them. The rangers were still a vital asset to the British army, and Rogers still enjoyed the full confidence of the senior commanders in the theater.

In the meantime, Lord Loudoun had been recalled, and was replaced by his second in command, James Abercrombie, another Scotsman. The deputy to any commander is an important role, and Abercrombie is said to have performed it well under Lord Loudoun. Whether this meant he was ready to become the new commander, however, was and continues to be up for debate. Hindsight shows us that even if he was a master of logistics, he did not have the strongest force of character or drive, to be revealed only in the splatter of blood.[113]

SCOUTING FOR AN INVASION

As spring turned to summer, the campaign season had once again come around. While the British fought through present-day Western Pennsylvania and the Maritime Provinces of Canada, Abercrombie planned to accomplish what Lord London had not: an invasion of Canada from the south. The forces gathering at Fort Edward were up to the task, both in quantity and quality. But first, the forts along the great warpath had to be taken in order to ensure safe passage and a secure supply line.

Rogers sent out multiple forces of scouts from Fort Edward to scout out enemy positions and to take prisoners for interrogation if possible. The most successful mission was led by Captain Jacob Naunauphtaunk's (known to Rogers and in this work hereafter as Captain Jacob) Stockbridge Ranger force, which met a force of seventeen men gathering wood. Ten were captured, while the seven who resisted were killed and scalped. It was not long before French-allied Native Americans returned the favor, ambushing Ensign Etowaukaum's force from Captain Jacob's company, killing and capturing several rangers.[114]

Rogers then received notice to start marshaling his forces in anticipation of Abercrombie's upcoming campaign against Fort Carillon. After the losses suffered at the Battle of Rogers Rock, no man could be spared. In early June, Lord Howe arrived with his force at Fort Edward and at once ordered Rogers to send a scouting force to prepare a map of the valley with its roads and defensive points. Rogers led the mission himself and was accompanied by about fifty men, including Captain Jacob, Lieutenant Noah Porter of Brewer's Company and Ensign Downing of the Fifty-Fifth Regiment of Foot.[115]

The scouting party proceeded to the ruins of Fort William Henry on Lake George with whaleboats carried in wagons. They then took the boats up Lake Champlain, landing on the east side of the Ticonderoga River. Leaving the boats and most of the rangers with Jacob and Downing, Rogers dispatched Porter and three Mohegan rangers to scout close to Fort Carillon while he and three others hiked up Rattlesnake Mountain (present-day Mount Defiance). Offering commanding views of Ticonderoga and its approaches, this mountain played an important role in history.[116]

After Rogers and Porter left, Captain Jacob and his party were attacked on three sides by a couple dozen French and Native American warriors. It was stated later that Jacob and his Native American rangers retreated immediately while the White rangers withdrew in good order, but who exactly fought well and who ran is hard to determine. Rogers was just returning from his mapmaking expedition and was able to skirt the French flank and make it back to the boats before Jacob and the others embarked. Five rangers were killed and three captured, including Ensign Downing.[117]

Porter heard the action and likely thought that the French were present in superior numbers. He decided to work his way around the battle and return to Fort Edward by a landward route. On the way, he encountered Lord Howe and his force and informed his superior that "Rogers must either be killed or taken." They were greatly relieved when Rogers and his men did return in their whaleboats on June 17.[118]

Portrait of John Bradstreet by Thomas McIlworth. He was the logistical master of the St. Lawrence and Mohawk theaters. *Courtesy of the National Portrait Gallery, Smithsonian Institution.*

At a debriefing with General Abercrombie, the rangers' accounts were made complicated by the arrival of the French Lieutenant Wolfe, who had led the ambush against Jacob and arrived under a flag of truce to discuss a prisoner swap. Abercrombie scolded Rogers in front of Wolfe for withdrawing too soon, but fortunately a tongue lashing was all he received. Despite the fiasco, the intelligence-gathering mission had been a success and the planned reduction of Fort Carillon could proceed.

The plan for the movement of the army and its implementation were left in the capable hands of Lieutenant Colonel John Bradstreet. Abercrombie was fortunate to have such a capable logistician serving under him. To move this force from the ruins of William Henry to Sabbath Day Point, he had assembled "a thousand bateaux and two hundred whaleboats." These would haul the British regulars and American provincial units, supplies and even artillery, all on a vast scale. In hindsight, such a force might have seemed like a miniature eighteenth-century D-Day armada moving under sail and oar power on a picturesque American lake.

Starting on July 5, 1758, the army moved twenty-five miles up the lake via a flotilla of boats. Pretending to encamp for the night, the army then slipped farther up the lake about four miles from Fort Carillon. They met a French force that quickly fled in the face of the overwhelming odds arrayed against them. The column continued with Rogers and his rangers in the vanguard, while the rest of the force was split into four columns. Lord Howe led the fourth column of colonial troops and rangers.

Bernetz Brook

Feeling that they still had the advantage of both time and surprise, Lord Howe decided to press ahead with his force and keep the French on the back foot. By taking the west side of the La Chute River, his force would be able to bottle up the French in the Ticonderoga peninsula. Rogers' Rangers were sent to secure a crossing at Bernetz Brook (present-day Trout Brook) and later reinforced by Connecticut provincials. A few hours later, they were followed by skirmishers from the Eightieth Regiment of Foot, then Israel Putnam's Connecticut Rangers and other provincial regiments.[119]

Howe's decision to send the rangers farther ahead of his force rather than at their van (the very front) would have consequences. The rangers had secured a ford on the Bernetz, but there was now a gap in between them and the Eightieth. Into this gap wandered a French force that had become lost trying to return to Fort Carillon. They had righted themselves on finding Bernetz Brook and planned to follow it to the La Chute River and then safety. Neither side was aware of the other's presence until they were nearly on top of each other.[120]

The forward part of the French force under the infamous Ensign Lagny challenged the Connecticut provincials, and on hearing an English accent, they opened fire, to which the Connecticut and Rogers' men immediately replied. On the opposite side of the French force, the skirmishes of the Eightieth leading the rest of Howe's force began to enter the fray. The French and the British had been surprised, but the former was now sandwiched between the forces of the latter.[121]

Lord Howe hastened to the sounds of the guns along with his brigade-major, Captain Alexander Monypenny" of the Fifty-Fifth. Just when he crested a hill and came upon the skirmish, he was shot through the chest. He was likely dead before he hit the ground, having been shot through the heart and spine. As he lay there, his hand quivered for an instant, and then he lay still. Though the French party was routed, it would later seem to many that the British had lost much more.[122]

Lord Howe had charisma, and though he was only the deputy commander of the army, it had been his zeal that breathed energy into the campaign. Mirroring his sudden loss was an equally sudden loss in inertia, and a malaise seemed to settle over Abercrombie and his force. Thomas Gage of the light infantry became the new deputy commander, though he did not seem to make any kind of impression on the campaign. Indeed, at the start of the American War of Independence, Gage, who was then commander-in-chief of the North American forces, once again failed to make any kind of impression on the fast-paced events that led to the separation of the colonies. Had Howe, who respected and was respected by his colonial counterparts, survived, perhaps things may have been different. The young general's death served as a harbinger of things to come, both near and far.

In the meantime, the rangers and provincials revenged themselves of the loss at Rogers Rock. Though fifty of the French force were able to escape thanks to the intervention of some of Montcalm's Grenadiers, the rest of the force was doomed, with about 150 killed and about the same amount captured. Still, the sudden sharpness of a bush fight had stopped the remaining British columns. Without Howe to lead them, the British failed to continue their drive into Montcalm's forces.[123]

FORT CARILLON

Of course, despite Howe's death, the campaign continued. A scouting party was sent to the summit of Mount Defiance (also known as Rattlesnake Mountain and Sugar Loaf Hill) to survey the French positions and make recommendations to Abercrombie. The party was composed of Captain James Abercrombie, aide and possible nephew to the commander, the engineer Lieutenant Matthew Clerk and an escort of rangers under Captain John Stark.[124] Also, a column of five thousand men was sent down the portage road under the command of the batteauman John Bradstreet.[125]

Bradstreet's men met no opposition, and they seized what was left of the ruined sawmills and began repairing the bridge over the La Chute. He requested permission to press on toward the fort but was denied by Abercrombie. Even a day after Lord Howe's death, such a move might have caught the French before their defenses were ready and another opportunity was lost.[126]

Also on July 7, the scouting mission of Captain Abercrombie and Lieutenant Clerk was carried out. Atop Mount Defiance, they could see the French at work on the defenses and were not impressed. They did not realize that they were only seeing the outer parts of the abatis, due to distance and camouflage that Montcalm had placed to hide the main works—a tactic much more successful than any of the French could have imagined.[127]

Here, at the Heights of Carillon, Montcalm had constructed a field fortification known as an abatis. This was a kind of breastwork or wall built of nature, with "layers of trees cut down, their tops facing outward, their branches interwoven." In safety behind this structure stood the French regulars and Canadian militia. Therefore, any attacking infantry marching in line or column would have its formation broken up by the felled trees and then try to bypass it all while under fire.[128]

The French forces were made up mostly of the eight battalions of regulars from France, with a small component of Troupes de la Marine and Canadian militia, with Native American forces being "virtually absent." Montcalm was known for his disdain of his Native allies and fought the battle with the forces he knew and trusted. However, given that they would be fighting a defensive battle in European fashion, he had the right kind of troops in the right positions. All he could have asked for was more men.[129]

Early on July 8, a group under John Bradstreet was sent in close to the French lines to either corroborate or contradict the assessment of Clerk and Captain Abercrombie. Getting close to the outer defenses, but what they

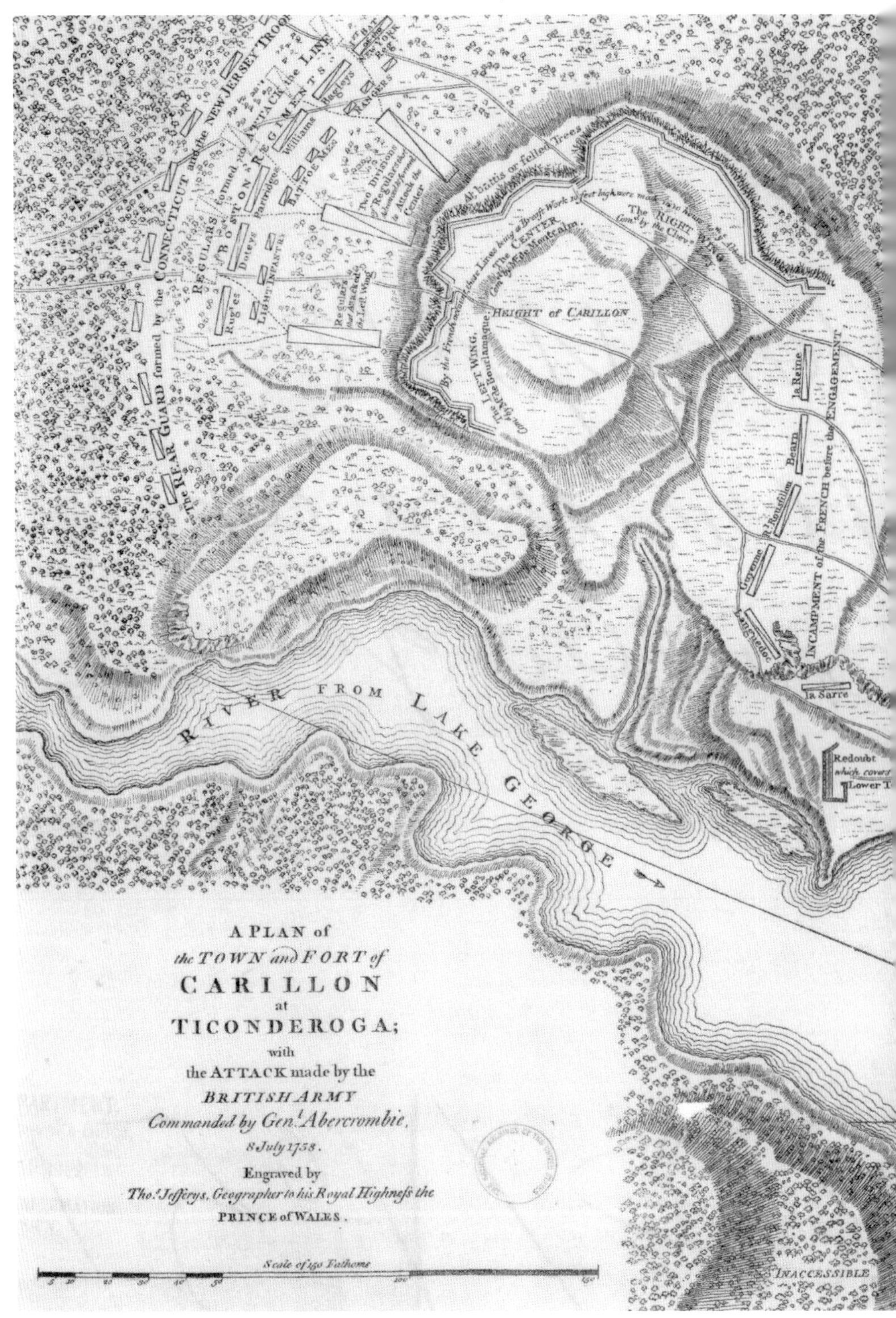
A PLAN of
the TOWN and FORT of
CARILLON
at
TICONDEROGA;
with
the ATTACK made by the
BRITISH ARMY
Commanded by Gen.l Abercrombie,
8 July 1758.
Engraved by
Tho.s Jefferys, Geographer to his Royal Highness the
PRINCE of WALES.
RIVER FROM LAKE GEORGE
HEIGHT of CARILLON
The REAR GUARD formed by the CONNECTICUT and the NEW JERSEY TROOPS
RANGERS
INCAMPMENT of the FRENCH before the ENGAGEMENT
la Reine
Bearn
la Sarre
Languedoc
Redoubt
INACCESSIBLE
Scale of 150 Fathoms

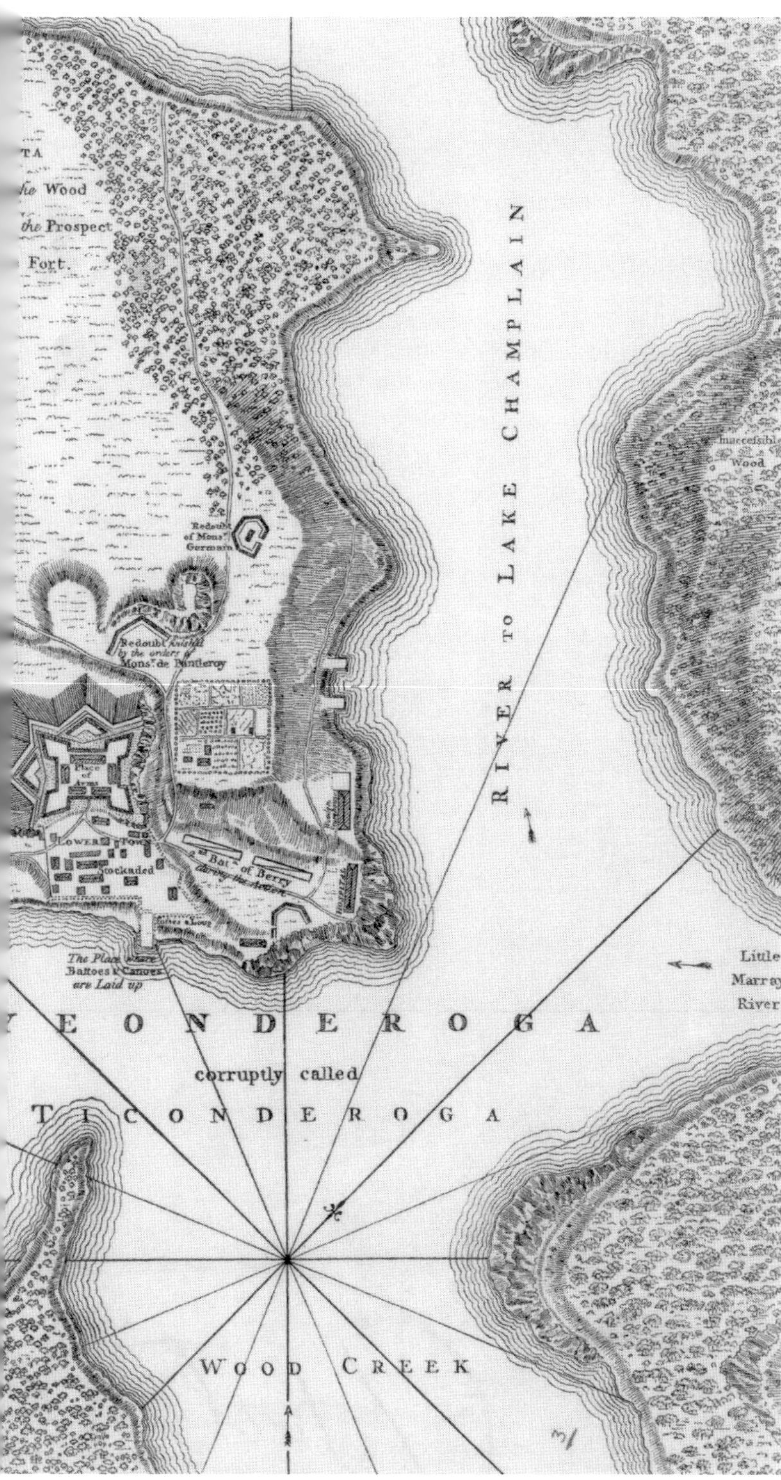

"A Plan of the Town and Fort of Carillon at Ticonderoga; with the Attack made by the British Army Commanded by Gen. Abercrombie." *Courtesy of the War Department Map Collection, National Archives.*

thought was the main French line, they came to the same conclusions as the earlier observers. At a council of war, Abercrombie made the decision that the French defenses were to be stormed that day.[130]

The attack was a classic frontal assault: skirmishers scattered their French opposites, and then the British regulars, being Abercrombie's most disciplined troops, made a direct advance on the French defenses in three lines of attack. They were followed by the provincial regiments behind them. Clerk, the engineer, recommended that a battery of artillery be placed on the south bank of the La Chute to support the attack.[131]

The skirmishers, including all the rangers, the batteaumen and the Eightieth Light Infantry, began their attack in the later part of the morning. Adaptive as ever, Rogers' men used the French abatis to their advantage, using it as a miniature woodland to snipe and pin down the enemy from, possibly even wounding Montcalm's aide, Louis-Antoine de Bouganville, who went on to become a famous explorer. Still, a few lucky shots were not enough to oust the French from their positions.[132]

The regulars began their assault in the early afternoon, including parts of the Twenty-Seventh, Forty-Second, Forty-Fourth, Forty-Sixth, Fifty-Fifth and Sixtieth Regiments of Foot. The Forty-Second Royal Highland Regiment of Foot, more popularly known as the "Black Watch," is the unit that won the most fame for its bravery and losses in the coming assault. Characteristic of most of the assault by the regulars, they marched toward the breastworks as ordered. But before they could reach it, their lines were muddled and broken by the downed trees and logs of the abatis, all

Line art drawing of an abatis, an obstacle formed of the branches of trees laid in a row, with the tops directed toward the enemy. *Courtesy of the Archives of Pearson Scott Foreman & Wikipedia.*

while taking volley after volley of French fire. The Black Watch and other regiments attacked time and again but with the same tragic result, especially for the Scottish Highlanders, who suffered a 65 percent casualty rate.[133]

General Jeffrey, First Baron Amherst. He led British and Provincial forces to victory in North America. *Courtesy of the Miriam and Ira D. Wallach Division of Art, Prints and Photographs: Print Collection, New York Public Library.*

If Lord Howe had lived, perhaps he might have managed a breakthrough or another strategy to save the day. Abercrombie remained behind the lines at the ruined sawmill and had no direct command over what was happening, becoming a bystander rather than a leader. He saw his men when they retreated at the end of the day, covered by Rogers' Rangers, who prevented a rout. Montcalm, thanks primarily to British blundering, had achieved a great victory.[134]

The blame for the disaster was pushed on the engineer, Lieutenant Clerk, who was conveniently not able to defend himself as he had been killed in the battle. Perhaps the last casualty of the campaign was to be General Abercrombie, who was sacked and replaced by a veteran recently returned from battlefields in Germany, Major General Jeffery Amherst. Though he had been serving on the other side of the world during the previous years of the Seven Years' War, he was a master of planning and logistics and would be able to build on his predecessors' work to finish the job of subduing New France.[135]

Through the rest of the year, the rangers of Moses Brewer's Company likely participated in scouting expeditions and patrols throughout the theater. Burt Loescher wrote that Noah Porter resigned from the company at the end of 1759, but it is more likely that he did so at the end of 1758. The company had a new first lieutenant (most companies had only one) in the spring of 1759, and he was certainly back in Charlestown by that summer. He was replaced in his position by John Fletcher. Mohegan warriors Joseph Duquipe and Joseph Johnson also resigned and were replaced by

Joshua Locke and George Turner, respectively; an ensign was also added in Benjamin Hutchins. These changes were rough on the company, as in the spring of 1759, twenty-two rangers of the company deserted, in addition to the previously mentioned clerk Lawrence Ekins.[136]

The year 1759 would come to be known throughout Great Britain as the *annus mirabilis*, the "year of miracles." The year saw the capture of Forts Carillon (Ticonderoga) and St. Frederic (Crown Point) on Lake Champlain. General James Wolfe achieved martyrdom on the Plains of Abraham and in doing so captured the bastion of Quebec, with some of Rogers' Rangers being present. Victories were also achieved in India, in continental Europe and at sea. The French were hard-pressed to recover from these setbacks.

In the meantime, the other Porter brothers continued the settlement of Charlestown and took turns manning the fort. In August 1759, William Heywood wrote in his journal, "William Porter and another man came here from Crown Point and said they left Captain Stark's and 120 men yesterday designed for this place." It is possible that William was assisting Stark in

The death of General Wolfe at Quebec. Note the soldier in either ranger or other irregular uniform standing above the Native American warrior. *Courtesy of the Miriam and Ira D. Wallach Division of Art, Prints and Photographs: Print Collection, New York Public Library.*

his task of building a road from Crown Point to Charlestown. After this event, William Porter seems to have disappeared from historical records. It is possible that he died or that he moved and his history was not recorded in his new abode. In 1752, he had acknowledged the paternity of a child born to Deliverance Walker, named William Walker Porter, who apparently later settled in Vermont.[137]

Men associated with No. 4 who went on active service throughout the war included the unfortunate Phineas Stevens, who died while in service in the Atlantic provinces. Two of his sons, Samuel and Simon, served in the rangers, the former becoming infamous while the latter saw much service under Wolfe at Quebec. Humphrey Hobbs, who was renowned for his service in the last war, also became a captain in the rangers, and his knowledge of the lands both east and west of New Hampshire was greatly valued. Like many others, he died of smallpox at Fort William Henry in the winter of 1756–57.[138]

St. Francis Raid

In August 1759, two British officers were sent to St. Francis under a flag of truce in order to "negotiate," though they were also carrying correspondence for Wolfe, who was besieging Quebec. The Abenaki handed the officers over to the French, with one reportedly being tortured. This offense proved to be the final straw, and Amherst ordered Robert Rogers to take his rangers and destroy St. Francis.

During King George's War, raiders from St. Francis had burned the farm of Rogers' family. But Rogers was not the only New Englander with a score to settle with St. Francis. Those frontier families that had not lost family members or property had lived in a kind of fear that such things might happen to them. Native Americans at St. Francis formed a collective bogeyman for the frontier Americans, whether real or imagined. It had long been an idea of Rogers to attack St. Francis and stop Abenaki raids at their source.[139]

Rogers sailed from Crown Point in a flotilla of whaleboats with nearly two hundred rangers, including Native American scouts, on September 13, 1759. They were forced to lie low near the mouth of Otter Creek due to the presence of a small squadron of French ships. While there, Rogers lost nearly a quarter of his force due to physical incapacity or accidental wounds. The force that proceeded to St. Francis probably numbered fewer than 150 men.[140]

Not long after landing at Missisquoi Bay, his boats were discovered by enemy warriors, and Rogers knew there was no way of returning the way they had come. Instead, they planned to return by Lake Memphremagog and the Connecticut River to Charlestown. He therefore sent some lame rangers back to Crown Point, with orders to ask Amherst to send Lieutenant Stevens at No. 4 to meet Rogers at Wells River (the northeastern-most point in present-day Newbury) with supplies. It would be a close-run thing, but if the players performed their roles, the journey home would be a successful one.[141]

Lieutenant Samuel Stevens was the son of the famous Captain Phineas and had spent much of his life in and around the Fort at No. 4. When commissioned into the rangers, Rogers had recommended to Amherst that he be placed in charge of the twenty rangers stationed at the fort, likely thinking that no one was better for the job than the son of its illustrious founder. By the time of the St. Francis raid, he had been in the post for much of the year.[142]

Stevens was ordered by General Amherst to receive provisions and "competent men" from Colonel Benjamin Bellows II, the commissary officer at No. 4, to supply Rogers and 170 men. These were to be taken to Wells River, about halfway between Lake Memphremagog and Charlestown, and Stevens was to remain there "so long as you think there is any probability of Major Rogers returning that way." He was to return the supplies or what remained of them to Bellows and then proceed to Crown Point. Amherst had left the duration of the time spent at Wells River to Stevens' discretion, a decision that would have fatal consequences for many.[143]

The men Bellows assigned to Stevens were Benjamin Sawyer, Enos Stevens and Noah Porter, most recently a lieutenant in the ranger corps. Little is known of Benjamin Sawyer, but Enos Stevens was yet another son of Phineas Stevens and as such was the brother of Samuel, who was leading this expedition. Enos was captured by Native Americans at the close of King George's War and taken to Montreal, but when the conflict ended, he was quickly released and came home via Albany.[144]

Farther north, Rogers had reached his destination after a difficult trek. After nine days travel through a swamp (which helpfully hid their movements from any pursuers) and fording a river using a human chain, the rangers were at St. Francis. Getting close to the settlement proved easier than expected, as most of the town's warriors were out serving on the front lines. These frontiersmen, having feared raiders from this place (real or imagined) for so long, must have felt great satisfaction at arriving at the enemy's doorstep for a surprise attack.[145]

October 4, 1759, was a dark day for the Abenaki of New France. With the element of surprise, Rogers' men attacked from the southeast and north, effectively pinning the inhabitants to the riverfront. Those at St. Francis mostly lived in French European–style buildings rather than traditional shelters, but they proved to be just as vulnerable to what was coming. Operating in pairs, the rangers moved from house to house, killing the warriors or others they could find, all the while setting fire to the town. About forty Abenaki men and women were killed in combat, in the flames of burning homes or shot while trying to escape; Rogers lost one Stockbridge ranger.[146]

Aside from those killed, the Western Abenaki suffered the loss of one of their largest villages, something not easily replaced. There are some who say that the attack was genocidal or an example of ethnic cleansing. Amherst, who ordered the raid, has since become notorious for his proposal to give Native American tribes smallpox blankets in an early example of biological warfare—perhaps a tactic not seen since the catapulting of plague victim corpses in medieval European sieges.

Rogers justified the raid by the hundreds of scalps he claimed to have seen hanging in the village. The provinces of New England rejoiced, more ecstatic over the event than the fall of Louisbourg and Quebec to Wolfe. This event, more than any other, made Rogers and his rangers into American legends, most notably depicted in the novel and Hollywood film *Northwest Passage*, starring Spencer Tracy as Rogers. Rogers personally helped elevate the events he and his men partook in with the postwar publishing of his memoirs and a book about the different lands and cultures of North America.

The Abenakis proved resilient, and though their population dwindled, they have survived. The fact that Missisquoi did not suffer the ravages of war helped them; when on the retreat from the failed 1775–76 Invasion of Canada, Joseph Powers, a future brother-in-law of Noah Porter, passed through the village. He found a flourishing settlement; though sources state that this occurred in 1760, he would have been only ten at that time, making it more likely it was while he was serving with New Hampshire troops in 1776.[147]

Surprise was achieved against St. Francis, but now the whole region knew they had been here. It was time for the rangers to get back to British territory as soon as possible. Supplies taken from the town kept the rangers and their captives fed for the eight-day journey south back to Lake Memphremagog.

There, to have better chances of hunting game, Rogers divided the men into nine parties of fifteen to twenty men each. They would meet again at Wells River, where Lieutenant Stevens was expected with supplies from the Fort at No. 4.[148]

About a week after Rogers burned St. Francis, the Stevens brothers, along with Sawyer and Porter, set out on their supply mission. No. 4 was the most northerly British position on the Connecticut River, so the men were operating behind enemy lines, or at least in the no-man's-land between New England and New France. A couple of days later, they reached Cohass but found the current too strong to proceed to Wells River by water, so each day they proceeded by land to look for and attempt to signal Rogers with gunshots.[149]

After several days of marching to Wells River and meeting none but a party of hunters, Stevens believed that Rogers was not coming and decided to head back downriver with the supplies in tow. When Rogers and his men came upon the scene of Stevens' camp, they found only the remains of a fire, having missed the relief party and all the food supplies they had by just a couple of hours. The hunger, despair and rage felt by Rogers and the others must have been unfathomable.[150]

On the return march, things became beyond desperate for Rogers and his men. When flora or fauna failed them, they were forced to eat parts of their shoes and belts and "broil their powder horns." Some men ate the flesh left on the scalps of the Abenaki they had taken, while others were forced to cannibalize their dead comrades. As the men had broken up into small parties, they met varied fates, including being killed or captured by the French or their allied warriors, eaten by wolves or lost to starvation and or the elements.[151]

One group of thirty-five rangers was "exterminated" near Missisquoi, and some others were taken prisoner. One group of five rangers was discovered with an Abenaki woman in a tow and the flesh of a child they had killed for food. The two carrying the human flesh were killed on the spot while the three others were taken prisoner. Rogers lost about 30 percent of his force from all these causes.[152]

As no supplies were waiting for them, Rogers and a couple others were forced to speed down to No. 4 and then bring back the supplies that should have been waiting for them. This they did, but they were too late for a couple dozen rangers who had died of starvation in the meantime. It is perhaps fortunate that Stevens was on his way to Crown Point when Rogers arrived in Charlestown, as there is no telling what kind of encounter might have happened. But even when all the rangers had made it down the river and filled their stomachs, they did not forget what they viewed as such a great betrayal by Stevens.[153]

After the raid, Noah Porter remained as a civilian at No. 4 through the winter and spring. In February 1760, he witnessed a sale of land from Simon Sartwell to Abel Walker. Walker was Porter's commanding officer in the Revolutionary War. He signed as a witness with the title "Noah Porter, Lieutenant," reflecting his past rank in the rangers and perhaps a present one in the garrison at Charlestown.[154]

However, by April, Porter was called to Crown Point at the request of General Amherst. On the way, he might have encountered Otter Creek for the first time. It was during the war, either as a ranger or civilian at an unknown time, that Noah Porter first came upon the river, which empties into Lake Champlain in present-day Addison County, Vermont.

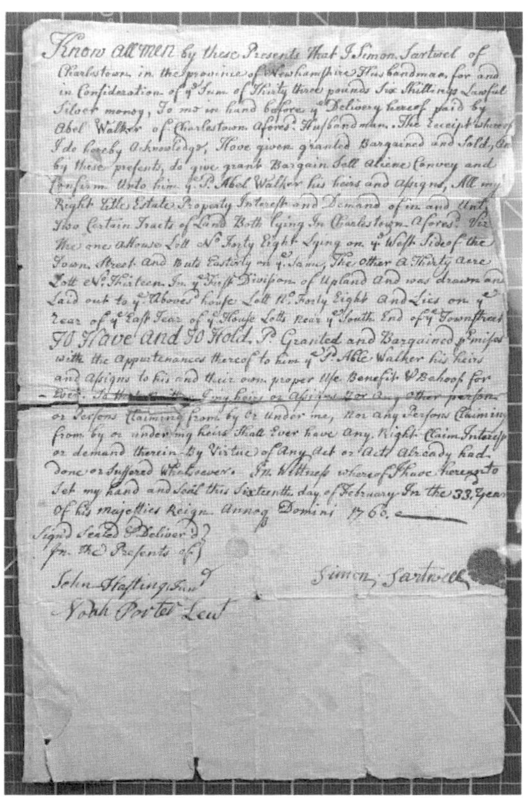

Know all men by these Presents that I Simon Sartwel of Charlestown in the province of New hampshire Husbandman, for and in Consideration of ye Sum of Thirty three pounds Six Shillings Lawful Silver money, To me in hand before ye Delivery hereof paid by Abel Walker of Charlestown afores.d Husbandman. The receipt whereof I do hereby Acknowledge, Have given granted Bargained and Sold, & by these presents, do give grant Bargain Sell aliene Convey and Confirm Unto him ye Sd Abel Walker his heirs and assigns, All my Right Title Estate Property Interest and Demand of in and Unto Two Certain Tracts of Land Both lying In Charlestown Afores.d Viz The one a House Lott No Forty Eight Lying on ye West Side of the Town Street and buts Easterly on ye Same, The other a Thirty acre Lott No Thirteen In ye First Division of Upland and was drawn and Laid out to ye Aboves.d house Lott No Forty Eight and Lies on ye rear of ye East Tear of ye House Lotts near ye South End of ye Townstreet To Have and To Hold, Sd Granted and Bargained premises with the appurtenances thereof to him ye Sd Able Walker his heirs and assigns to his and their own proper Use Benefit & Behoof for Ever. [illegible] my heirs or Assigns Nor Any other person or Persons Claiming from by or Under me, Nor any Persons Claiming from by or under my heirs Shall Ever have Any Right Claim Interest or demand therein By Virtue of Any Act or Acts Already had done or Suffered Whatsoever. In Witness whereof I have hereunto Set my hand and Seal this Sixteenth day of February In the 33 Year of his majesties Reign Annoq Domini 1760.

Sign.d Sealed & Deliver.d
In the Presents of

John Hastings Jun.r
Noah Porter Lieu.t

Simon Sartwell

Simon Sartwell's deed for sale of land in Charlestown, New Hampshire. Witnessed by Noah Porter, his signature indicates he could possibly read and write. *Courtesy of the Rauner Library Archives and Manuscripts Collection at Dartmouth University.*

George Washington Porter related how his grandfather "once said that he crossed Otter Creek, in one of those years, with a scouting party on the rocks at the head of the falls…and he and his party were so impressed with the wild and chaotic features of the scene that they spent some time in viewing the falls. He said the west channel appeared very small and was so filled with flood-wood that you would hardly notice there was any channel there; that there were several beaver houses built on the flood-wood."[155]

It was only that preceding fall when the falls and outlets of Otter Creek were mapped and detailed by the rangers and other scouting parties. The man charged with doing so Captain Noah Johnson, perhaps the oldest member of Rogers' Corps. He had fought with Lovewell at Pequawket in Dummer's War, served during King George's War and was a member of Rogers' original company. He died of wounds received the summer before Rogers' raid on St. Therese.[156]

Porter was impressed with Otter Creek, an area that would play an important part in his life. But on his arrival at Crown Point, he had more pressing matters to attend to. With the dust settled after the raid on St. Francis, Rogers was determined that Lieutenant Stevens should be punished for his actions. A court martial was convened on the orders of General Gage, with the president being Major Archibald Gordon of the Twenty-Seventh (Inniskilling) Regiment of Foot, who interviewed the deponents on April 3. Stevens and all the men he took with him to Wells River ended up testifying, including Noah.

> *Noah Porter sworn, deposes, that on or about the 13th of October last he with Lieut. Stephens of the Rangers, and four more men embarked in a canoe with provisions in order to meet Major Rogers and his party (returning from a scout) at Cohass at which place they arrived on the 19th and about the 20th he heard three or four shots fired from the north east quarter, in a little time afterwards a batteau appeared with two men in it, that were hunting, who told them they had been firing guns, that they stayed until the 23rd in the evening, being three days, during which time some of the party went every day to Well's River, but seeing nor hearing nothing of the Major or his party they returned and got to No. 4 in three days being 26th October.*[157]

The other men varied somewhat in their descriptions of dates and durations, but for the most part, the testimonies matched. There are some then and now who say Stevens should have at least left the supplies behind, but that would have directly contradicted Amherst's orders. No matter what anyone said though, the plain fact was that Stevens had left too early, and for that it was the will of Amherst and Rogers that he be punished at least in some way.

Stevens was cashiered from the rangers in disgrace and returned to Charlestown. Fortunately for him, his fortunes fared better after the war. He became a surveyor and a leading man in Charlestown, serving in several town government positions and as a colonel in the militia before dying in 1823 at age eighty-nine. The fact that he became a Patriot while Rogers became a Loyalist likely helped his later reputation.[158]

The Surrender of Montreal

In the months after the St. Francis raid, little went well for the French in North America or through the rest of the world. Now came the final campaign for New France, with a march to the beating heart of the colony: Montreal. Joining Rogers in this campaign was Noah Porter, who had re-enlisted in Rogers' own company on August 11, 1760.[159] He made his way to Crown Point, now a massive British military camp, via the road Stark had cut through the wilderness the preceding year. Though he was no longer an officer (and never would be again), he still saw much to gain by participating in the victory campaign against the French.[160]

The invasion force he joined (there were three coming from different directions and converging on Montreal) was composed of 3,500 soldiers and 600 rangers led by General William Haviland, one of Rogers' and Porter's enemies among the British regulars. The army left Crown Point on August 16, sailing up Lake Champlain and then the Richelieu River via bateau and canoe. After weathering storms, the fleet landed about a mile south of their first objective, the French stronghold of Isle au Noix. Though the garrison numbered only about 1,600 (mostly militia), it held control over the river and would have to be taken to proceed farther north.[161]

For over a week, the British tried to cut through the log booms blocking the river under intense cannon fire but made little progress. Rogers was ordered to haul several cannons through the woods and was able to sneak up on the French ships guarding the booms. After a brief cannonade, the squadron was routed, with several vessels being captured. Seeing their naval forces lost, the French withdrew from their fort and retreated north. Rogers was now given the task of chasing their heels.[162]

Rogers and his men sailed north in one of the vessels they had captured, catching up with the French rear guard and skirmishing with them successfully. He was finally stopped when a French force more than twice their size turned on them, and they were forced to disengage. The rest of the French force was able to get into Montreal, but it was not enough to delay the inevitable. The city was surrendered to the British, and with it went New France. The war between Great Britain and France in their North American colonies was over. Going forward, Canada would be a British possession.

The Surrender of Detroit

Adventures were still to be had for Noah Porter. Amherst gave Rogers new orders to proceed west, to accept the surrender of French outposts, especially that of Detroit. Rogers was ordered to take two additional companies with him, but it seems unlikely he proceeded without his own company, of which he was both captain and major. These men, including Porter, were his chosen men, and it seems unlikely he would not have taken them with him.[163]

They set out that fall by canoe, proceeding along the St. Lawrence and then Lake Ontario, then carried their boats into Lake Erie. Rogers took some of his men to Fort Pitt (present-day Pittsburgh, Pennsylvania) to link up with General Robert Monckton and collect some regulars to take with him to Detroit. Rogers met with Native American leaders along the way (including the soon-to-be-famous Chief Pontiac) informing them of the French capitulation and that the British were now the masters of this part of North America. They arrived at the Detroit River at the end of November, finishing what historian John Ross called "the longest and fastest expedition taken in British colonial North American history."[164]

Upon turning over the letters he carried with him to the French commander at Fort Detroit, Rogers received the surrender of the post peacefully. He also took and garrisoned Fort Miami (present-day Fort Wayne, Indiana) and Fort Ouiatenon (present-day West Lafayette, Indiana). Rogers personally planned to take a lieutenant and couple dozen men to Fort Michilimackinac, located along the Straits of Mackinac, which connects Lake Michigan and Lake Huron.[165]

Rogers attempted the journey, but the winter conditions of mid-December forced them to turn back to Detroit. He did not waste his time there, though; mixing personal business with that of the British army, he purchased thirty thousand acres of land in Michigan from the Chippewa tribe. Then, Rogers, likely with his own company in tow, returned to Fort Pitt, arriving on January 23, 1761. From there, Rogers proceeded to Philadelphia, his journey at an end.[166]

Rogers saw service in Pontiac's War, published his journals and a book about North America and attempted an expedition to look for the fabled Northwest Passage. His reputation was tarnished when he was tried by a military court on the accusation that he was acting as a French spy. He was acquitted but was not able to receive a full commission in the British army or the East India Company. Living on half-pay, he even spent time in a London debtors' prison. Up to the start of the American Revolution, little went right for him.

His Majesty's Independent Company of Rangers served under Rogers through Pontiac's War as well. When that conflict ended and a period of relative peace came over North America, their services were no longer needed. There was no definitive conclusion to their service; like old soldiers, they simply faded away. For a unit that had undergone so many evolutions and growth spurts, it is perhaps not surprising that this occurred. But so long as Rogers lived and sought service (mostly futilely) with the king, the idea of the unit stayed alive in the minds of British colonists.

No doubt, the rangers were an important asset to the Crown as they waged a woodland war half a world away. But in terms of success, they often fell short of their French counterparts. Though they prided themselves on being manhunters, they had twice been ambushed themselves on a large scale with horrendous losses. And though French and Native American raiding parties had come near Albany, Rogers and his men had mostly patrolled Lakes George and Champlain, with their raid on St. Francis being their most daring thrust into the enemy's heartland; victory in this war came not so much through their skill but in the crushing superiority of numbers that the British and provincials brought forth. Still, to the victor goes the spoils, including the legend in this case.[167]

The rangers may have disbanded, but their deeds and the legends surrounding them certainly live on. Perhaps the most tangible part of their legacy was one born in the Second World War. When the U.S. Army sought to emulate the British commandos who had "set Europe ablaze," as Churchill had asked them to, they developed a force that trained with the former. Seeing the similarities between their independent nature, hit-and-run tactics and ability to conduct amphibious warfare, General George Marshall named the new force the U.S. Army Rangers.[168]

Noah Porter returned to Charlestown after his second enlistment, and on October 1, 1761, he married Lois Powers. Now that the war was over and the Abenaki and other tribes were no longer military threats, he and the others from No. 4 could return to their settlement across the Connecticut River, attempting to maintain and expand what they had started. It took on even more importance, as it was located along the newly built road from Crown Point to Charlestown. The question now though was whether it really was theirs at all.[169]

There is an expression that says "possession is nine-tenths of the law," but such a maxim can get muddled when you look at the early history of what became Springfield, Vermont. Noah Porter; his wife Lois' family, the Powers; and the Sartwell families were on the land, working it and transforming it into something useful. But legally they were squatters and did not have the funds to purchase their homes and farms. They petitioned Governor Benning Wentworth of New Hampshire for land grants but were ignored.[170]

In that fall of 1761 in Northampton, Massachusetts, a group of proprietors met to plan the future of the town. They had been given a charter to the town by Governor Wentworth, likely because they were able to pay him while the squatters could not. They visited the settlement already begun, but what relationship they had with the squatters is not known. By the next year, these men under Gideon Lyman were parceling out the land and voted to eject those squatting on it.[171]

This was easier said than done, and things had become more complicated by 1764. King George III ruled that the Connecticut River was the boundary between New York and New Hampshire, and therefore the governor of New York viewed the grants issued by New Hampshire as voided. Gideon Lyman and the other proprietors applied for the same grant from New York, but not much was resolved in the following years. In the meantime, the squatters continued to reside at Springfield, but Noah Porter at least thought that it might be good to have a backup plan.

In 1766, he along with some other fellow rangers applied for two thousand acres of land each, to be located on the east side of Lake Champlain, where, in an area not known for it at the time, the land was more suited to farming.[172] It seems that this was not granted, as eight years later in 1774 he applied with ex-rangers William Barron, Joshua Locke and David Stone for the same amount of land in "Totten and Crossfield's Purchase" on Schroon Lake. In November the following year, a survey of the properties was registered as completed, but by then the provinces of North America had become a very different place.[173]

In the meantime, he was more successful where he was, as he served as a commissioner of highways for the Town of Springfield in 1769. As the town had no select board or council at the time, it seems that these commissioners served as a kind of governing body. In 1771, he is listed as living in Springfield in the census of the New Hampshire Grants.[174] By 1772, Porter and others had reapplied for land grants in Springfield on the same basis of squatters' rights. It is not known how New York replied to them, but it seems their claims were further disputed by Phineas Lyman.[175]

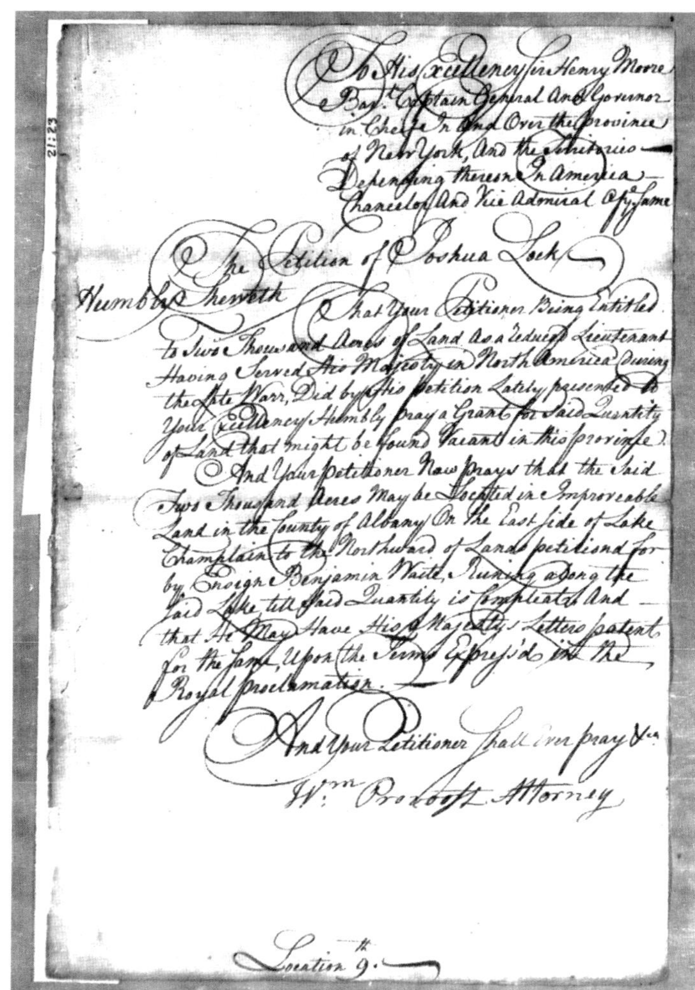

To His Excellency Sir Henry Moore Bart. Captain General and Governor in Chief In and Over the Province of New York, and the Territories Depending thereon In America Chancellor and Vice Admiral of ye Same

The Petition of Joshua Lock

Humbly Sheweth

That Your Petitioner Being Entitled to Two Thousand Acres of Land as a reduced Lieutenant Having Served His Majesty in North America During the Late Warr, Did by His Petition Lately presented to Your Excellency Humbly pray a Grant for Said Quantity of Land that might be found Vacant in this province.

And Your petitioner Now prays that the Said Two Thousand Acres May be Located in Improveable Land in the County of Albany On the East Side of Lake Champlain to the Northward of Lands petitiond for by Ensign Benjamin Waite, Running along the Said Lake till Said Quantity is Compleated And that He May Have His Majesty's Letters patent for the Same, Upon the Terms Express'd in the Royal proclamation.

And Your Petitioner Shall ever pray &c.

Wm. Prevoost Attorney

Location 9th.

These are to Certify to all whom it may Concern, that Lieutenant Noah Porter, hath Served in America during [th]e War, and was Disbanded at the conclusion thereof.

Given under my Hand at Head Quarters in New York, this 25th Day of January 1766

Thos. Gage

Top: Application for Land Grant by Lieutenant Noah Porter, completed by an attorney on his behalf. *Courtesy of the New York State Archives.*

Bottom: Certificate of Lieutenant Noah Porter's Military Service, signed by General Thomas Gage. *Courtesy of the New York State Archives.*

Noah Porter remained in the Springfield-Charlestown area through much of the upcoming American Revolution and War of Independence, though unlike his brother James at No. 4., it seems that he failed to establish any kind of permanent "legal" settlement at either place. Having seen the lands that lay northwest in the New Hampshire Grants, he knew that good land was still out there waiting to be claimed. Soon, he would no longer have to ask the British authorities for permission to take it.

8

THE AMERICAN WAR OF INDEPENDENCE

Frontiers of Democracy

The American War of Independence began with the "shot heard 'round the world" at the Battles of Lexington and Concord on April 19, 1775. The British force, seeking to confiscate supplies that might be used in rebellion against them, marched to Concord. Stopping to confront the militia force on the green at Lexington, a sudden musket shot led to an exchange of fire, and the militia fled. The British then proceeded to Concord, where they burned what few items of contraband they could find. Thinking the rising smoke meant the town was being burned, Patriot militia stormed the North Bridge, and this time, it was the British that fled. After a fighting withdrawal to Boston, the rebel militias of Massachusetts and it neighbors proceeded to surround and lay siege to the city.

In June, to hinder the British use of Boston Harbor, a Patriot force was ordered to fortify Bunker Hill on the Charlestown Peninsula. The Americans worked through the night and into the morning, and the sounds of their picks and shovels carried down to the British ships in the harbor. Unfortunately, the Americans had constructed their redoubt on Breed's Hill, more forward than Bunker Hill and thus more exposed. Seeing this new position in the light of day, the British immediately resolved to remove the rebels from it.

Among the British opponents in Boston were General Thomas Gage and General William Howe, brother of the late Lord Howe who was killed at Bernetz Brook. Now William was the direct commander in an assault on the same populace who had purchased a memorial for his brother at Westminster Abbey. Also present was Lieutenant Colonel James Abercrombie, who had

Top: Portrait of General Thomas Gage by John Singleton Copley. *Courtesy of the Paul Mellon Collection, Yale Center for British Art.*

Bottom: General Israel Putnam. Famed for his service in the Connecticut Rangers, he was one of the commanders at Bunker Hill. *Courtesy of the Miriam and Ira D. Wallach Division of Art, Prints and Photographs: Print Collection, New York Public Library.*

served as an aide to his namesake uncle, who had commanded Anglo-American forces at the disastrous Battle of Carillon.[176]

Tracking the movements of individuals over two centuries after these events took place is difficult. It is made especially more difficult when two individuals share the same name and come from the same town. Such was the case with Noah Porter and the son of his brother James, his nephew Noah Porter. This work will attempt to untangle the two from confusing paper trails and give both their due.

Noah's brother James and his son Chandler were reportedly at Bunker Hill as minutemen serving under Stark, but this fact is only listed in a secondary source (albeit perhaps from an oral history) and not found in any surviving muster rolls; his brother-in-law Joseph Powers was also at Bunker Hill with the Third New Hampshire Regiment.[177] There was a Noah Porter who served in Woodbridge's Regiment of Militia from Hampshire County. This was likely James's son Noah, as the elder Noah signed a document pledging Cumberland County's support with New York in the new crisis at Springfield on July 26, 1775, and was thus not in Boston at the time.[178]

Though General Artemas Ward commanded the Americans at the siege of Boston, the command structure on the peninsula was more complicated. Former Connecticut ranger Israel Putnam was commanding from Bunker Hill nearer Boston, while Samuel Prescott was commanding forces more forward and in the newly built structure atop Breed's Hill. It would be some time before this was truly a "continental" army, and the militiamen mostly took orders from only those they knew and trusted, especially friends, neighbors and family members.

Being one of the units selected as reinforcements, John Stark's and John Reed's New Hampshire Regiments marched to where they were needed. Even though Charlestown Neck was swept by the fire of nearby British warships, Stark marched his men at a deliberate speed, saying that one fresh man in the battle was worth ten tired ones. Having had experience in fast-paced small unit actions in his last war, no doubt Stark knew what he was talking about.[179]

Stark paused near Putnam on Bunker Hill, but if any words were exchanged between the two old rangers, history does not record them. Stark realized that the best position for his men would be on the American left flank, extending the American line to the Mystic River. The men were put behind a rail fence, which they reinforced with all they could find to try to increase levels of cover, and Stark placed an aiming point fifty yards in front of his men. They were joined by Reed's Third New Hampshire Regiment on their right, and there they waited for the regulars to come.[180]

Howe sent his light infantry against the New Hampshire men on the American left, along with the Fourth, Tenth and Twenty-Third Grenadier Battalions. When the Twenty-Third reached Stark's marker, his men fired, routing the light infantry, who left nearly one hundred casualties behind. The grenadiers were forced to pull out of range and reform in order to properly conduct their attack. Stark's experience and leadership had held the American left.

Major General John Stark as he looked later in life. Like Putnam, his service in the rangers likely helped his rise to top command. *Courtesy of the Miriam and Ira D. Wallach Division of Art, Prints and Photographs: Print Collection, New York Public Library.*

Meanwhile, Noah Porter the younger was likely experiencing much fighting himself. Woodbridge's Massachusetts Regiment was split between the redoubt on Breed's Hill and the buildings in Charlestown. The redoubt, being the highest position and the central point of resistance, was the main target of the British. They made multiple frontal assaults against it and several times were repulsed. The units in Charlestown used the buildings and barns as cover to skirmish and snipe at the British forces, though they were gradually pushed back while doing so.[181]

If young Noah was in the redoubt, he was lucky to escape with his life. Despite one last volley by Prescott's men, the British stormed the ditch and despite heavy losses bayoneted their way into the redoubt. Prescott ordered a retreat, and those who could fled, sometimes on their hands groping their way out through the thick smoke. Dr. Joseph Warren of the Sons of Liberty was killed when it fell, his body repeatedly bayoneted by the vengeful British.[182]

Inevitably crushed by overwhelming force, the redoubt on Breed's Hill fell and the Americans took flight to Charlestown Neck. Stark's men were performing well and were prepared to counterattack the British Light Infantry, but he saw that he would be left behind and had a more important role to play. His men retired in good order, covering the retreat of the American force, like the job the rangers had performed after the disaster at Carillon.[183]

Among the British casualties was Major John Pitcairn of the Royal Marines, who was one of the leading officers at Lexington and Concord. Ironically, also killed was Colonel Abercrombie, who had advocated for a similar frontal assault against the abatis at the Battle of Carillon nearly two decades earlier. The British had won the field and retained control of Charlestown Peninsula, but it was a Pyrrhic victory. If they were to sustain such losses in each action with the Americans, it would not be a war worth fighting.[184]

A Fork in the Road

While Putnam and Stark made themselves heroes of a budding nation on hills overlooking Boston Harbor, Robert Rogers was still at sea, returning to America after a six-year absence. His main goal was to look for the fabled Northwest Passage, and he had no comprehension of the momentous events occurring on his native soil. He was forced to sign a nonaggression pact in Philadelphia. And from New York to Portsmouth, New Hampshire, where his wife and son lived, he was being watched closely. While he may have just been going from colony to colony to settle his finances, he was naive in not realizing that this activity by a British officer on half-pay might have looked like intelligence gathering.[185]

Having been thrown out of New York City, Rogers visited Portsmouth again, where it seems Betsy threw him out as well. He would not see his wife or son, Arthur, ever again, with New Hampshire later granting her a divorce. Trouble followed him to New Jersey, where he was arrested on the orders of General George Washington. When the two met, Rogers insisted he was on his way to offer his services to America. Washington did not believe him and recommended that he be denied an officer's commission. Jailed in Philadelphia, Rogers soon escaped, making his way to British lines, his allegiance having been chosen for him.[186]

Fortunately for Rogers, Thomas Gage was sent back to England after the disastrous victory at Bunker Hill, so he no longer had to face a hostile commander in chief. He was commissioned as a lieutenant colonel and given the task of recruiting a force of Loyalist rangers by General William Howe, to be called the Queen's Rangers.[187]

While doing so, he exposed schoolteacher Nathan Hale as a Patriot spy, leading to the latter's arrest and execution. The Queen's Rangers raided well but also met their match against Continental forces. In an overhaul of the militia, Rogers was relieved of command. His life declined from this point, as he drank and sank further into debt. His part as a player on the North American stage was at an end.[188]

The Battle of Bennington

Having repulsed the attempted American invasion of Quebec, the British now planned to combine their forces in Canada, and those under General Howe that had recently taken New York City, to use the "great warpath" to sever the rebellious colonies of New England from the others, to divide and conquer the rebellion. Howe was supposed to march his force north, but this plan was never put into action. But General John Burgoyne was ready to take his army south down the Richelieu River to Lake Champlain. The British now had the same hand that those in New France had hoped to play two decades earlier.

Burgoyne launched his campaign in the summer of 1777 in a thrust down the Champlain Valley not dissimilar to one made by Montcalm. The first step in the campaign was retaking Fort Ticonderoga. Learning the lessons of the bloody Battle of Fort Carillon, the British placed artillery on Mount Defiance, making Ticonderoga extremely vulnerable and forcing its evacuation. It is ironic that the fortress that had supplied the cannon that had lifted the Siege of Boston had also been made untenable in the same manner. The British army scattered the Continental forces before them and moved into upstate New York. The campaign was achieving success, but with each mile marched came more challenges.[189]

Any army moving deeper into enemy territory and away from its main supply bases is confronted with logistical problems. Increased distance means more moving parts to the supply machine, and if these begin to slow down, the invasion force does as well. Burgoyne's army, reliant on a finite number of horse- and ox-drawn wagons for supplies, began to lose momentum. It was decided to send a predominantly German force under

Lieutenant Colonel Friedrich Baum into Vermont and New Hampshire to gather supplies and wreak what havoc they may.[190]

With this force was a force of men from the Queen's Loyal Rangers, commanded by Captain Justus Sherwood. Sherwood had been one of Ethan Allen's Green Mountain Boys but disagreed with them over the war with Great Britain. After he and his family were threatened by their former compatriots, he fled to Canada and threw in his lot with the British. He later acted on behalf of the British to try to get the Vermont Republic to leave the war with a British guarantee of independence, though he was obviously unsuccessful in that venture.[191]

The Vermont Republic called on its neighbors for aid, and New Hampshire answered the call with a militia force to be commanded by former ranger John Stark. Stark had led a distinguished career in the war to this point, but after being passed over on the promotion list, he resigned and returned to New Hampshire. He accepted the command of this force on the condition he be answerable to New Hampshire alone, rather than his former Continental army superiors.[192]

Stark's influence, as well as the idea of an approaching British force and advanced pay being offered, stirred the men of the state to action. He quickly put together a militia force of nearly 1,500, about 10 percent of the adult male population of New Hampshire at that time. Following preparations at the Fort at No. 4 and reinforcements from other quarters, the force marched to Bennington.[193]

Marching with the force was former ranger Noah Porter, who was serving in Captain Abel Walker's Company (the captain himself being a neighbor to the Porter family in Charlestown) in Colonel David Hobart's Regiment of Militia. He had marched with this company before when it had marched to support Fort Ticonderoga when Burgoyne began his invasion, then as part of Benjamin Bellows III's regiment. The company turned around on hearing that Ticonderoga had fallen. Noah's brother James, who had helped defend the Fort at No. 4 in 1747, was in this unit, as was his son Chandler; they had been captured during that expedition. Now this company marched again, and Porter had returned along with several brothers-in-law and possibly other kinsmen.[194]

Both sides converged toward Bennington in present-day Vermont. After some skirmishing, Baum's force dug in near Walloomsac, New York. There, concerned about the size of the American force against him, he ordered the construction of several redoubts, made up of trenches and earthworks reinforced with logs. Burgoyne sent word to Baum that he could hold where he was if he felt threatened but not to withdraw until he received orders to do so. In the meantime, he had dispatched reinforcements to him. Following orders, Baum decided to hold tight in his small forts.

Stark held a council of war to plan the attack. He had taken part in a frontal assault at Fort Carillon in 1758 and watched the British suffer severe losses at Bunker Hill more recently; he had no desire to repeat the folly of those attacks. He therefore decided to divide his force into three groups and assault Baum's redoubts from all sides. The Anglo-German force would be forced to divide their fire and hard pressed to reinforce any faltering sections. It was a good plan, but it required good timing, surprise and a firm hand of leadership. Fortunately for the militia, Stark was not another James Abercrombie.

On August 16, 1777, battle was joined at Walloomsac. Stark sent parts of his forces to the left and right to flank Baum, while Hobart's and Stickney's regiments were to storm the "Tory Redoubt" and made a demonstration in front of the enemy. This deployment was like the one later used by the famous King Shaka of the South African Zulu Kingdom, known then as the "buffalo horns." No doubt Stark had taken Rogers' rules to heart and managed to deploy his forces to strike at the enemy from most all sides.

Stark led his men with a cry: "There's the enemy, boys! We must flog them, or Molly Stark sleeps a widow this night." The New Hampshire and Vermont forces took the "Dragoon Redoubt," with those who did not manage to escape being captured or killed, the latter category including Baum.[195] A quick victory here was certainly a boon, but a tougher fight was still going on in the Tory Redoubt.

Here, the Loyalists could be seen "fighting to the last like tigers" against their former neighbors. As would be seen in the American Civil War as well, former compatriots divided by different ideals can fight even more bitterly than strangers thrown into a war zone. But though the Tories fought bravely, "they were completely surrounded within their fortifications, and the work of death was finished with bayonets and clubbed muskets. Hobart's and Stickney's men saw the work thoroughly done." Those who survived in this redout joined their German and British comrades in captivity.[196]

As the prisoners were being rounded up across the battlefield, another Hessian force entered the fray. Stark, his force still recovering from the last action, might have been hard-pressed to take on this challenge alone. Fortunately, Colonel Seth Warner's Regiment of Green Mountain Boys arrived at the same time. Engaging Warner and then Stark, this reinforcement

The Battle of Bennington by Don Troiani. This excellent work shows the fighting at close quarters that occurred in the "Tory Redoubt." *Courtesy of the U.S. National Guard.*

force was forced to make a fighting withdrawal, finally escaping under the cover of night.[197]

Stark and Warner had won the day, having demolished one enemy force and putting the other to flight. As the fighting was so furious, it seems surprising that Captain Walker's Company had none killed or mortally wounded. It is possible they were one of the lesser engaged companies in Hobart's Regiment, perhaps even in reserve, or that with men like Noah Porter and his brothers-in-law the Powers brothers, they simply out-fought their opponents.

In total, the Battle of Bennington cost the British 200 dead and 700 captured of a total force of 1,400 engaged, a catastrophic casualty percentage.[198] It also contributed to the American victory at Saratoga, with Burgoyne surrendering the entirety of his army. This victory was instrumental in getting official French support for the war effort. No doubt the Porter brothers (including the likely recently released James and his son), who had fought their fair share of battles against the French and their allies, must have found it quite an interesting turn of events.

The New World Made New

Following Burgoyne's defeat at Saratoga, the northern colonies no longer had to fear a large-scale British invasion from the North, though the war did continue in this area. Noah Porter, some of the Powers boys and other No. 4 men served time in the garrison at the newly recaptured Fort Ticonderoga in early 1778. But even though the British had abandoned Ticonderoga, they still maintained a presence on Lake Champlain and in the newly christened Vermont Republic especially, which, as mentioned earlier, they tried to turn against the other American colonies.[199]

Lasting victory came in 1781 with the victory of the Patriots and their French allies over the British at Yorktown, Virginia. The war was ended by the 1783 Treaty of Paris, and the British and Hessians vacated the newly independent United States of America. Those who had chosen the side of the rebellion could now reap the rewards of lands no longer under British control, if not a monetary compensation from the new government. Loyalists, who had chosen to remain loyal to their monarch, were forced to leave their lands forever, and many were forced to ask the British government for help.

Joshua Locke, fellow ranger and would-be neighbor of Noah Porter of Lake Champlain, chose to remain loyal like his old commander of the rangers and faced the consequences. He served with the British when they took New York in 1776 and later tried to raise a unit of Loyalists at his own expense. He left for England upon the cessation of hostilities and was forced to write to the British home secretary asking for financial relief. Living in London in the late 1780s, his final fate is unknown.[200]

The last few years of Robert Rogers' life remain murky to most historians. Having to live a life in exile due to his choice to be a Loyalist, he had no prospects and drank his meager allowance from the British army away while living in London. He died there in 1795, an impoverished alcoholic, and his grave site has sadly been lost. His brother James moved to Canada after the war, and Rogers' own son, Arthur, left descendants in New Hampshire.[201]

After the War of Independence, the militaries of Europe and the United States were far less reliant on rangers in their forces. The light infantry that was a fledgling force under Gage in the French and Indian War had grown in importance in the British military and took on the role of skirmishers; though it may be argued that the British army failed to truly appreciate this sort of tactic until the bloody lessons of the Second Boer War. Still, the green jackets of Britain's famous riflemen of the Napoleonic Wars may remind an observer of the uniforms of Rogers' Rangers. As for scouting, light cavalry and dragoon units were able to perform this task in more open ground. Their ability to scout, raid and forage in enemy country would be most prominent in the American Civil War. Still, for wilderness like that found in New York and Vermont, no unit could have done a better job than the rangers or their French adversaries.

After his second war, Noah Porter finally got to the land he so desired on Lake Champlain at Ferrisburgh, Vermont, in the early 1780s, where he went to hunt and trap. He settled on about forty acres of land beside the lake and Otter Creek that came to be known as "Porter's Borough." It's ironic that the western mouth of the waterway that had served as a highway for French and Indian raids into New England was now owned by this former ranger: to the victor went the spoils.[202]

He seemed to have a rocky start in Ferrisburgh, as the town asked him and his family to leave in 1787, an act usually done when a family was so poor that the town would have to support them. His children were listed as Nathan, Lovina, Versel, Lois, Louranny, Noah Junior and Laura. Despite this event, the family stayed and apparently had more success, and Noah became a respected figure in town, even if he was nearly fined for "striking Edward Gould."[203]

Noah Porter served as a surveyor of highways for several years and at one time served as the town's tithing man. A holdover from earlier Puritan times in New England, the tithing man made sure that no one skipped church on the Sabbath, that everyone behaved during services, and that the congregation donated as often and as much as they should. With a man as formidable as Noah holding this job, it is likely that all went smoothly for the church that year.[204]

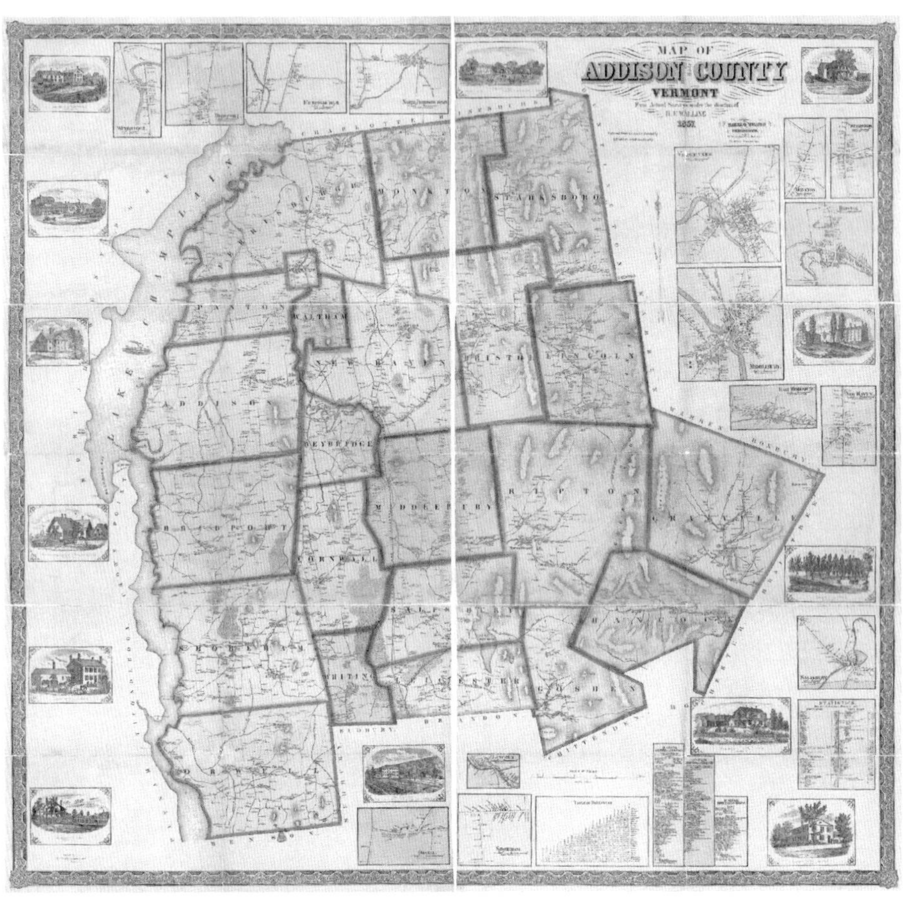

Map of Addison County, Vermont. Ferrisburgh and Vergennes can be seen in the northwest corner. *Courtesy of the Library of Congress, Geography and Map Division.*

9

THE WAR OF 1812

THE LAST BATTLE FOR LAKE CHAMPLAIN

Noah Porter may have finally found the land of his dreams, but he had not yet escaped war on the American continent. Though the Native Americans had long since stopped calling it such, the Champlain Valley was still very much the "great warpath," and it was not long before Porter and his family literally had a battle unfolding in their very own backyard.

In early 1800s, tensions over trade, economic dealings with France and impressment of American sailors to fight with the Royal Navy against Napoleon led to a breakdown in relations between the United States and Great Britain. What came to be known as the War of 1812 was just another theater of the Napoleonic Wars to the British Empire, but to America it meant defending the country's honor and its rights.

Noah Porter was now far too old to march to war (though he may have fought if the enemy marched to him), but his children supported the war effort, either in and out of the military, both man and woman. The youngest, Noah Wright Porter, served with William Sumner's Regiment of Vermont Militia. Versel Porter is said to have served with the Green Mountain Volunteers and raised the rooster that became famous at the Battle of Plattsburgh, but no records have yet been found by the author to substantiate these claims. The daughters of Noah did what they could to help the soldiers and sailors defending Vermont.[205]

It was one of the goals of the U.S. War Department to launch an invasion of Canada, whose position as a British colony meant it was still a volatile neighbor decades after the War of Independence. It may have even crossed the minds of some American politicians that Canada might be annexed as a new U.S. state or even multiple ones. But to launch a successful invasion up north or defend against one, naval superiority first had to be achieved and maintained on the Great Lakes and Lake Champlain.

The man appointed to the Champlain squadron was Lieutenant Thomas Macdonough. He started his service in the so-called Quasi-War with Revolutionary France and served under Commodore Stephen Decatur during the Barbary Wars. He was part of the crew of the ketch *Intrepid* when they sailed into Tripoli Harbor to burn the captured U.S. frigate *Philadelphia*, an act England's famous Lord Horatio Nelson called "the most bold and daring act of the age."[206]

Macdonough, who had been commanding gunboats at Portland, Maine, finally arrived at Vergennes, Vermont, in October 1812. Taking over from Lieutenant Sidney Smith, he had two sloops and two gunboats with which to fight and keep the lake and knew he would need more. By the end of the year, he had added one more ship, the sloop *President*, and continued to press his superiors for experienced men as they wintered in harbor.[207]

Macdonough moved his base several times, from Vergennes to Burlington and then Plattsburgh, New York. His squadron met with disaster in the spring of 1813 when his two sloops *Growler* and *Eagle*, under Lieutenant Smith, chased British gunboats too close to their base at Isle aux Noix and were captured. He was left with *President* and two gunboats.[208]

Portrait of Thomas Macdonough, commander of the U.S. Navy squadron on Lake Champlain. *Courtesy of the National Portrait Gallery, Smithsonian Institution.*

That summer, due to their newfound superiority, the British were able to launch raids on American towns along Lake Champlain, including Burlington and Plattsburgh. The American squadron was back at Burlington and successfully repelled the British, though achieving little beyond that. For this and prior service, Macdonough was promoted to the rank of master commandant.[209]

It was during the skirmish at Burlington that Macdonough first used the tactic of cabling his ships to the shore. When fresh men and guns on the other side of the vessel were needed to fight the enemy, the cables could be used to turn the ship (known as winding) in place rather than having to get underway and maneuver. Surprisingly, the British failed to see the danger in this tactic.[210]

In that summer of 1813, more sailors were received from the squadron, among them two who had enlisted in New York City, James Courtney and Reuben Sharpe. The latter was an Englishman who had absconded from the Royal Navy and was thus serving under the alias "Robert Gary," as capture by his former service would mean reinstatement into its ranks or much worse. They sailed up to Albany on a gunboat, then took a wagon to Whitehall, New York, and then a ship to Burlington, where they joined the *President*.[211]

By the winter of 1813–14, Macdonough had two more sloops of war, and he had also begun to build more on the Vermont side of the lake. Due to its position of comparative safety and access to the waterfalls on Otter Creek, Vergennes was selected as the site to build the new ships of the American flotilla. It had "a blast furnace, air furnace, eight forges, a rolling mill, a wire factory, a grist mill, and a mill for fulling cloth." It may have been in miniature, but the master commandant finally had his own shipyard, where he built two more gunboats and the twenty-six-gun ship *Saratoga*.[212]

Vergennes shared a border with Ferrisburgh, the town where at the mouth of Otter Creek (as stated earlier, it lay in Noah Porter's lands), which was adjacent to Porter Bay. When the new ships of the squadron sailed, this is where they entered Lake Champlain. As such, the American squadron kept its winter quarters in the mouth of the creek. An aged Noah Porter, who turned eighty that May, along with his family, found themselves on the front lines of a war between a fledgling American squadron and the mighty Royal Navy.[213]

As the home of Lois Porter, daughter of Noah, and her husband, Zopher Davis, was a "short distance" from the ships in winter quarters, sailors such as Courtney and Sharpe were "frequently" at their house during that winter. It is likely then that the two became acquainted with Lois and Zopher's daughters Lois and Polly Davis. On April 21, 1814, James Courtney and Polly were married by her uncle through marriage, the Reverand Oliver Alford.[214]

As the ice cleared from Lake Champlain that very month, Macdonough sought to prepare himself against a raid on his shipyard. One thousand Vermont militia were sent to defend Otter Creek, and a fieldpiece was placed on the ridge overlooking the mouth of the creek, likely on the Porter farm.

The peninsula at the mouth of the creek next to Porter Bay was armed with seven twelve-pound guns under the command of naval Lieutenant Stephen Cassin. Ten row-galleys were also stationed there.[215]

On May 14, 1814, the British arrived with one sixteen-gun vessel, five sloops, thirteen row-galleys and a bomb vessel. Commander Daniel Pring planned to sink two merchant sloops he had brought with him at the mouth of the creek to make navigation in and out of it impossible. It might then have been possible to have landed forces along the creek and march to Vergennes and wreak havoc at the shipyard. But before all this, the galleys and bomb vessel approached the mouth and tested the American defenses.[216]

For an hour and a half, they did so, but they did not get the results they wanted. They likely did not expect to find the Americans in such strength, and the British Commander Pring claimed, "Every tree on the Lake Shore seems to have a Jonathon stationed behind it," possibly including the sons and sons-in-law of Noah Porter. After much cannonading by both sides, the Royal Navy withdrew, having suffered one sailor killed and two marines wounded.[217]

The Mouth of Otter Creek at Ferrisburgh, Vermont. *Author photo.*

Lake Champlain's Porter Bay, at Ferrisburgh, Vermont. *Author photo.*

Whether an aged Noah or his family joined in the battle is unfortunately unknown, but one of his grandsons, George Washington Porter, was apparently near to the action at only about three years old. Despite his young age, he recalled "distinctly seeing the soldiers at the time of the attack of the British." No doubt they would likely have found spent artillery shells on their property or nearby from those that failed to hit the battery, as most seemed to do. The Americans hoped to get downriver to fight the British outside Otter Creek, but by the time the *Saratoga* was ready, the enemy had withdrawn. The two squadrons met again that fall, when the stakes were much higher.[218]

James Courtney and Reuben Sharpe both transferred from the *President* to the *Saratoga*, which became Macdonough's flagship as soon as it was completed. Courtney left the navy to live with Polly that summer when his year-long enlistment expired. Sharpe, likely after an appeal from the squadron's officers, chose to reenlist for a term of one year or until the aftermath of the battle with the British squadron. Due to his prior naval experience, he served as quarter gunner aboard the *Saratoga*, the rank of a petty officer responsible for four of the ship's guns and their crews.[219]

The British began their invasion of New York on September 1, 1814. Led by Sir George Prevost, the army was a formidable force mostly composed of veterans who had served under the Duke of Wellington in the Peninsular War against Napoleon. The New York side of Lake Champlain was chosen as not to interfere with the illicit food supply chain coming through Vermont. Prevost's force made it as far as Plattsburgh before he met serious resistance.[220]

Brigadier General Alexander Macomb had at Plattsburgh a force of regulars only a tenth of the size of Prevost's great army. This was doubled by militiamen from New York and Vermont, but the Americans were still outnumbered. Prevost planned to deal with Macomb, but after an American gunboat attack on his force, he waited for the Royal Navy to deal with the American squadron at Plattsburgh first. Newly led by George Downie, the British squadron included the powerful thirty-seven-gun frigate HMS *Confiance*, three other vessels (two of which had been captured from the Americans in 1813), five galleys and seven gunboats.[221]

Macdonough prepared his squadron for an attack, and the *Saratoga* was cabled to the shore as his other vessels had been in the battle at Burlington in 1813. He had three other vessels, then six galleys and four gunboats. Two other American vessels, including USS *President*, were away and did not take part in the action. The Americans formed a battle line facing north to south and awaited the British force. On September 11, 1814, the two fleets had their engagement.[222]

Early that morning, the British squadron bore down on the American line. Downie hoped to put the *Confiance* in a position to rake the *Saratoga*, in which a full broadside is delivered into the bow or stern of an enemy who has few or any guns to reply in that position. The Americans concentrated on the British flagship, which, due to ill winds, was forced to anchor "two cable lengths" from the American line. Even with a relatively inexperienced crew, the first broadside from the *Confiance* killed 20 percent of the *Saratoga*'s sailors.[223]

The two flagships exchanged broadsides, and fifteen minutes into the melee, Downie was killed by a dismounted cannon that fell on him. Macdonough was knocked unconscious twice, the first time by a splinter and the second by the decapitated head of one of his sailors. The smaller ships and boats joined the action at this time, and Lake Champlain was now the scene of a naval battle the likes of which had not been seen since Benedict Arnold was defeated at Valcour Island.[224]

Soon the British *Finch* was forced to surrender, and several gunboats were sunk. The American *Eagle* was forced to back away from the British fire, which in turn made the *Saratoga* and *Ticonderoga* more vulnerable. The *Saratoga* had suffered greatly in its battle against the *Confiance* and other vessels. All the starboard guns were now out of action. It was time for Macdonough to turn the flagship and with it the battle. The anchor and cables were used to

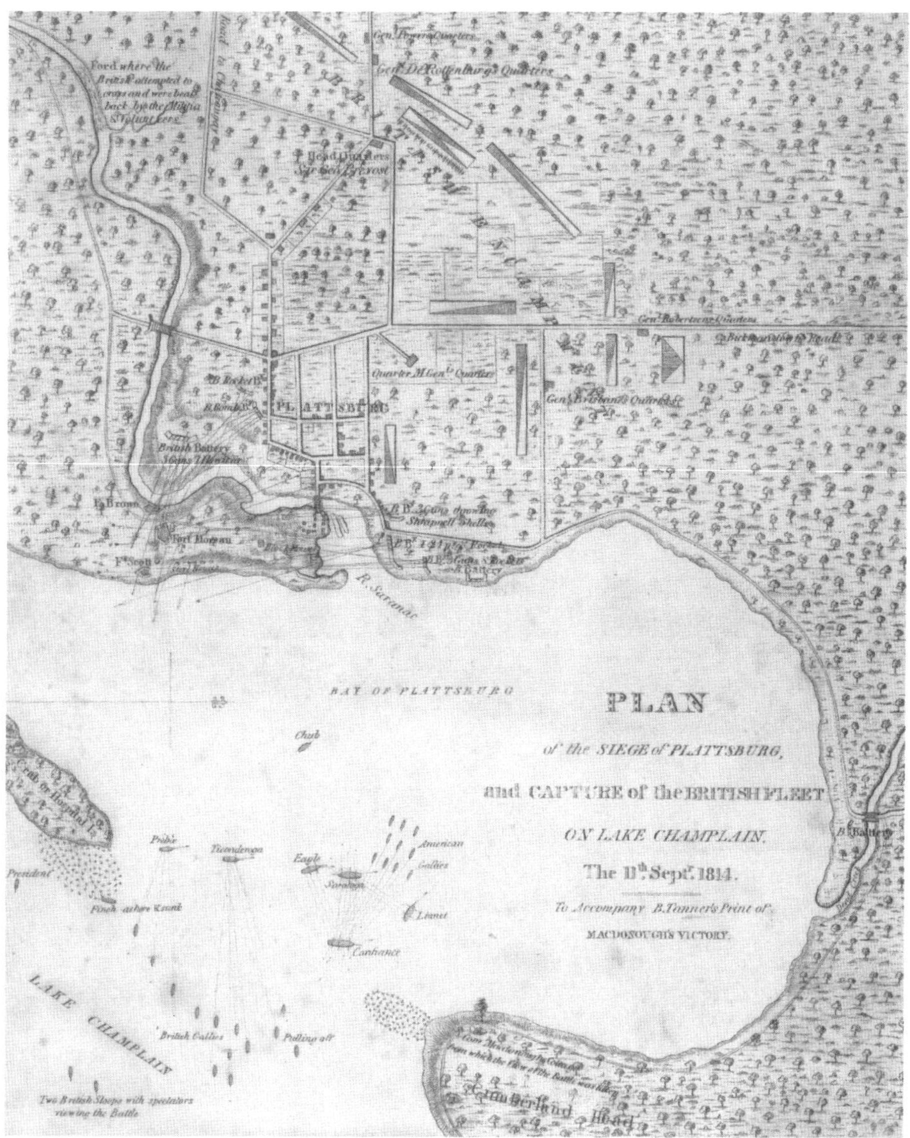

"Plan of the Siege of Plattsburgh and Capture of the British Fleet on Lake Champlain."
Courtesy of the Library of Congress, Geography and Map Division.

wind the vessel, and its fresh port side guns were brought to bear against the British flagship.[225]

While the *Saratoga* was being turned, Reuben Sharpe was wounded in the left thigh by a piece of "langrage shot" fired by the last remaining guns aboard the *Confiance*, either the last workable carronade or swivel gun. Langrage shot was like cannister shot, which was a canvas bag of small metal balls that spread out when fired from an artillery piece. It differed in that instead of using metal balls, it was metal junk—spent silverware, nails and any other unwanted metal. While Sharpe was also wounded in two other places, having a rusty nail blasted into your thigh in that time meant an infection at the least, death at the worst.[226]

Stunned by the fresh onslaught from the *Saratoga*, the *Confiance* attempted to turn in a similar manner, but its crew could not keep their stations under the withering fire. No more could be done, and the *Confiance* struck its colors. Pring in the *Linnet* kept fighting for twenty minutes, but then his ship was forced to give in to the fire of the *Saratoga*'s portside battery and the battle came to an end. The Royal Navy had lost the battle for Lake Champlain.[227]

"Macdonough's Victory on Lake Champlain and Defeat of the British Army at Plattsburgh by Genl. Macomb, Sept. 17th, 1814." *Courtesy of the Miriam and Ira D. Wallach Division of Art, Prints and Photographs: Print Collection, New York Public Library.*

Those who lived on Otter Creek could hear the booms of naval artillery echoing down the lake, roughly thirty-two miles away. Unfortunately, those there had no idea who had won or even who had survived. Wanting to know more, Zopher Davis and his son-in-law James Courtney left for Plattsburgh "a day or two" later. They searched for their friend and found Quarter Gunner Sharpe with his swollen thigh wound.[228]

The squadron under the late Downie had done their utmost to beat the Americans, but the same may not be said of Prevost. Though he was originally confident of victory, a change came over him after seeing the British squadron surrender. His force immediately began a retreat back to Canada, abandoning the invasion of the United States. This victory, combined with the defense of Baltimore and Fort Erie and finally Andrew Jackson's victory at New Orleans, helped America at the peace talks ending the war as equals. There were no territorial changes, and the War of 1812, with the last great campaign fought on the great warpath and in western New England, ended in 1815.[229]

According to family lore, Davis and Courtney brought Sharpe back to Otter Creek, where the family nursed him back to health—or as close as they could get with such a wound, which bothered him the rest of his life. Especially helpful was Lois Davis, who became dearer than the others to him. On October 16, 1814, Reuben and Lois were married by a justice of the peace at Ferrisburgh. The officiant likely would have been her uncle Oliver Alford, had he not left for lands in Erie County, Pennsylvania, that year.[230]

In 1816, Lois Porter Davis and her family followed her brother Nathan and sister Lovina and their family to northwest Pennsylvania. The children of Noah Porter had not ventured west before, and it is unlikely that they saw the Porter homestead on Otter Creek or their families there again. But though this was a daring trip, it is possible they heard of the area from their father, who might have visited Fort LeBoeuf fifty-six years before with Robert Rogers when the latter met Chief Pontiac. While his older brothers and sisters moved out west, Noah Wright Porter remained in Ferrisburgh, likely taking over his father's property on his death.

Noah Porter breathed his last on July 2, 1825. He was buried in the Porter Cemetery on the property he settled, and his grave remains there to this day, the stone weatherbeaten but erect. Notice of his death was published in newspapers and periodicals across the country. The *Rhode Island American* recorded the death of Noah Porter:

> *At Ferrisburgh, Vt., aged 93 years; 67 years ago he was a lieutenant under General Abercrombie and was attached to the column led by Lord Howe when that young nobleman fell; served in the Revolution as was perhaps the last survivor of that gallant army that attacked the works of Ticonderoga in 1758.*[231]

An abbreviated version of the obituary was published in the *Niles Weekly Register*, a periodical that recorded fascinating events, among other things. Before the epitaph was placed the following notice: "'the Last of the Mohicans,'" a new novel, by the author of the Spy, Pioneers, etc. is announced as in the press, shortly to be published, by Mr. Wiley, of New York."[232]

It seems fitting that perhaps the most famous work written about the French and Indian War made its debut shortly after the death of one of its most active participants. James Fenimore Cooper's most well-known work and its adaptations continue to enthrall audiences to this day, mythologizing the conflict that shaped the course of American and world history. And so, as so often happens, history passes into legend.

Grave of Noah and Lois Porter in the Porter Cemetery at Ferrisburgh, Vermont. *Author photo.*

NOTES

Prologue

1. Hall, *History of Eastern Vermont*, 71.
2. Ross, *War on the Run*, 47–50.
3. Chartrand, *Raiders from New France*, 26–27.

1. King Philip's War: Learning from the Masters

4. Schultz and Tougias, *King Philip's War*. This chapter relies heavily on this excellent work and is but a brief overview from these historians' fascinating and detailed history.
5. Lee, *Genealogical and Memorial History*, 1149.
6. Church and Drake, *History of King Philip's War*. For more on Church's expeditions to Maine, his son Thomas Church's biography goes into detail, biased as the source is.

2. King William's War: New France's War of Terror

7. Cohen, *Conquered into Liberty*, 22.
8. Cohen, *Conquered into Liberty*, 22.
9. Chartrand, *Raiders from New France*, 24–25.
10. Chartrand, *Raiders from New France*, 8–9.

3. Queen Anne's War: Carnage on the Connecticut

11. Calloway, *Western Abenakis of Vermont*, 103; Chartrand, *Raiders from New France*, 42–43.
12. Calloway, *Western Abenakis of Vermont*, 106–7.
13. Hall, *History of Eastern Vermont*, 71.
14. Stoutenburgh, *Dictionary of the American Indian*, 368.
15. Wells, *History of Newbury*, 511.

4. Dummer's War: Grey Lock versus Massachusetts

16. Connecticut Historical Society, *Papers and Reports*, 15.
17. Calloway, *Western Abenakis of Vermont*, 113.
18. Calloway, *Western Abenakis of Vermont*, 118; Temple and Sheldon, *History of the Town of Northfield*, 192.
19. Calloway, *Western Abenakis of Vermont*, 125; Stachiw, *Massachusetts Officers and Soldiers*, 199.
20. Saunderson, *History of Charlestown*, 523.
21. Massachusetts Births and Christenings, Ancestry.com.
22. Calloway, *Western Abenakis of Vermont*, 130.
23. Calloway, *Western Abenakis of Vermont*, 141–42; Saunderson, *History of Charlestown*, 14–17.
24. Saunderson, *History of Charlestown*, 19–20.
25. Saunderson, *History of Charlestown*, 19–20.

5. King George's War: Chasing Shadows

26. Ross, *War on the Run*, 36.
27. Ross, *War on the Run*, 36.
28. Ross, *War on the Run*, 43–44.
29. Calloway, *Western Abenakis of Vermont*, 144, 149.
30. Calloway, *Western Abenakis of Vermont*, 150–51.
31. Saunderson, *History of Charlestown*, 33–36.
32. Saunderson, *History of Charlestown*, 34–35.
33. Saunderson, *History of Charlestown*, 34–35.
34. Stark, *Memoir and Official Correspondence*, 373–74.
35. Stark, *Memoir and Official Correspondence*, 374.
36. Stark, *Memoir and Official Correspondence*, 374.
37. Calloway, *Western Abenakis of Vermont*, 155.
38. Heywood, "Unpublished Journal," notes taken by Barbara Jones of the Fort at No. 4, October 21, 2005, notes from Archive at Charlestown Historical Society, accessed December 8, 2023; Saunderson, *History of Charlestown*, 403.
39. MacKay, *Massachusetts Soldiers*, 357.
40. MacKay, *Massachusetts Soldiers*, 358.
41. Calloway, *Western Abenakis of Vermont*, 156–57.
42. Heywood, "Unpublished Journal."
43. Calloway, *Western Abenakis of Vermont*, 157; Saunderson, *History of Charlestown*, 53.

6. The French and Indian War, 1754–57: Bushwacked

44. Calloway, *Western Abenakis of Vermont*, 161–62.
45. Cohen, *Conquered into Liberty*, 2.
46. Cohen, *Conquered into Liberty*, 10.
47. Cohen, *Conquered into Liberty*, 10.
48. Calloway, *Western Abenakis of Vermont*, 162–64.
49. Calloway, *Western Abenakis of Vermont*, 164–68, 170, 172.
50. Zaboly, *American Colonial Ranger*, 7.
51. Ross, *War on the Run*, 2, 43; Loescher, *History of Rogers Rangers*, 3:2.

52. Ross, *War on the Run*, 78–79.
53. Ross, *War on the Run*, 73.
54. Ross, *War on the Run*, 113.
55. Locke, *Memorial of Joshua Locke*.
56. Rogers, *Journals of Major Robert Rogers*.
57. Cohen, *Conquered into Liberty*, 43–44.
58. Cohen, *Conquered into Liberty*, 81.
59. Cohen, *Conquered into Liberty*, 55–56.
60. Loescher, *History of Rogers Rangers*, 1:112–13.
61. FamilySearch; Loescher, *History of Rogers Rangers*, 1:113.
62. Loescher, *History of Rogers Rangers*, 1:118–21.
63. Loescher, *History of Rogers Rangers*, 1:122–23.
64. Loescher, *History of Rogers Rangers*, 1:122–23.
65. Ross, *War on the Run*, 128.
66. Ross, *War on the Run*, 128–29.
67. Ross, *War on the Run*, 132–33.
68. Loescher, *History of Rogers Rangers*, 1:113, 127.
69. Massachusetts, Town and Vital Records, 1620–1988; Loescher, *History of Rogers Rangers*, vol. 1.
70. Saunderson, *History of Charlestown*, 593–94.
71. Richardson, *Eighteenth Century Springfield*, 38.
72. Bates, *Rolls of Connecticut Men*.
73. Loescher, *History of Rogers Rangers*, vols. 1 and 3; also, various money converters on the internet, especially the British National Archives.
74. Rogers, *Journals of Major Robert Rogers*, 82–86.
75. Zaboly, *American Colonial Ranger*, 41.
76. Zaboly, *American Colonial Ranger*, 31.
77. Hall, *History of Eastern Vermont*, 72.
78. Zaboly, *American Colonial Ranger*, 9.
79. Ross, *War on the Run*, 163.
80. Ross, *War on the Run*, 189.
81. Loescher, *History of Rogers Rangers*, 1:116.
82. Zaboly, *American Colonial Ranger*, 58.
83. Ross, *War on the Run*, 163.
84. Zaboly, *American Colonial Ranger*, 9, 58
85. Zaboly, *American Colonial Ranger*, 48.
86. Zaboly, *American Colonial Ranger*, 60–61.
87. Loescher, *History of Rogers Rangers*, vol. 1; Rogers, *Journals of Major Robert Rogers*.
88. Loescher, *History of Rogers Rangers*, vol. 1.

89. Flavell, *Howe Dynasty*.
90. Loescher, *History of Rogers Rangers*, 1:201–2.
91. Loescher, *History of Rogers Rangers*, 2:200–2.
92. Zaboly, *American Colonial Ranger*, 45.
93. Loescher, *History of Rogers Rangers*, 2:205; Ross, *War on the Run*, 150–51.
94. Loescher, *History of Rogers Rangers*, 2:202–3; Ross, *War on the Run*, 151–52.
95. Loescher, *History of Rogers Rangers*, 2:304–8.
96. Loescher, *History of Rogers Rangers*, 2:304–8.
97. Loescher, *History of Rogers Rangers*, 2:309–11.
98. Cohen, *Conquered into Liberty*, 93.
99. Ross, *War on the Run*, 162.
100. Loescher, *History of Rogers Rangers*, vol. 2, 3:33.
101. Cohen, *Conquered into Liberty*, 26.

7. The French and Indian War, 1758–63: Britain Triumphant

102. Cutter, *Historic Homes and Places*, 623; Loescher, *History of Rogers Rangers*, vols. 2 and 3.
103. Loescher, *History of Rogers Rangers*, vol. 3.
104. Loescher, *History of Rogers Rangers*, 3:57.
105. Loescher, *History of Rogers Rangers*, 1:116.
106. Ross, *War on the Run*, 162–65.
107. Cohen, *Conquered into Liberty*, 74; Ross, *War on the Run*, 169–71.
108. Cohen, *Conquered into Liberty*, 74–75.
109. Ross, *War on the Run*, 174–77.
110. Ross, *War on the Run*, 177–80.
111. Ross, *War on the Run*, 180–84.
112. Zaboly, *American Colonial Ranger*, 14.
113. Cohen, *Conquered into Liberty*, 101.
114. Loescher, *History of Rogers Rangers*, 2:1–2.
115. Loescher, *History of Rogers Rangers*, vol. 3.
116. Loescher, *History of Rogers Rangers*, 2:3–5.
117. Loescher, *History of Rogers Rangers*, 2:3–5.
118. Loescher, *History of Rogers Rangers*, 2:3–5.
119. Chartrand, *Ticonderoga 1758*, 37.
120. Chartrand, *Ticonderoga 1758*, 41.

121. Chartrand, *Ticonderoga 1758*, 41.
122. Chartrand, *Ticonderoga 1758*, 41.
123. Chartrand, *Ticonderoga 1758*, 41–44.
124. Cohen, *Conquered into Liberty*, 106; Ross, *War on the Run*, xvii.
125. Chartrand, *Ticonderoga 1758*, 46.
126. Chartrand, *Ticonderoga 1758*, 45–46.
127. Chartrand, *Ticonderoga 1758*, 57–59.
128. Cohen, *Conquered into Liberty*, 97.
129. Cohen, *Conquered into Liberty*, 103.
130. Chartrand, *Ticonderoga 1758*, 59–60.
131. Borneman, *French and Indian War*, 135.
132. Zaboly, *American Colonial Ranger*, 20.
133. Chartrand, *Ticonderoga 1758*, 29; Borneman, *French and Indian War*, 136.
134. Borneman, *French and Indian War*, 138.
135. Cohen, *Conquered into Liberty*, 117–88.
136. Zaboly, *American Colonial Ranger*, 46; Loescher, *History of Rogers Rangers*, vol. 3.
137. Heywood, "Unpublished Journal"; Stark, *Memoir and Official Correspondence*, 447; Charlestown Town Records.
138. Loescher, *History of Rogers Rangers*, vol. 3.
139. Cohen, *Conquered into Liberty*, 72.
140. Loescher, *History of Rogers Rangers*, 2:57.
141. Calloway, *Western Abenakis of Vermont*, 177.
142. Saunderson, *History of Charlestown*, 568–69.
143. Loescher, *History of Rogers Rangers*, 4:199.
144. Loescher, *History of Rogers Rangers*, 4:198; Saunderson, *History of Charlestown*, 50–51.
145. Loescher, *History of Rogers Rangers*, 2:58–59.
146. Zaboly, *American Colonial Ranger*, 63.
147. Calloway, *Western Abenakis of Vermont*, 181; Hammond, *Rolls of the Soldiers*.
148. Loescher, *History of Rogers Rangers*, 2:60.
149. Loescher, *History of Rogers Rangers*, 4:196–98.
150. Ross, *War on the Run*, 264.
151. Zaboly, *American Colonial Ranger*, 42.
152. Calloway, *Western Abenakis of Vermont*, 177–78.
153. Borneman, *French and Indian War*, 232.
154. Dartmouth University, Simon Sartwell deed.
155. Smith, *History of Addison County*, 641.
156. Loescher, *History of Rogers Rangers*, 2:51–54; 3:12–13.

157. Loescher, *History of Rogers Rangers*, vol. 4, appendix 13.
158. Saunderson, *History of Charlestown*, 569.
159. Loescher, *History of Rogers Rangers*, vol. 2.
160. Loescher, *History of Rogers Rangers*, vol. 3; Ross, *War on the Run*, 286.
161. Ross, *War on the Run*, 286.
162. Ross, *War on the Run*, 286.
163. Borneman, *French and Indian War*, 258–59.
164. Borneman, *French and Indian War*, 258–59; Ross, *War on the Run*, 288, 300.
165. Ross, *War on the Run*, 306–7.
166. Ross, *War on the Run*, 310–11.
167. Cohen, *Conquered into Liberty*, 79.
168. Darby and Baumer, *Darby's Rangers*, 30.
169. Heywood, "Unpublished Journal."
170. Richardson, *Eighteenth Century Springfield*, 38–39.
171. Richardson, *Eighteenth Century Springfield*, 82; Hubbard and Dartt, *History of the Town of Springfield*, 4-8.
172. Cohen, *Conquered into Liberty*, 8.
173. Secretary of State of New York [NY], *Calendar of N.Y. Colonial Manuscripts*.
174. Holbrook, *Vermont 1771 Census*, 67.
175. Hubbard and Dartt, *History of the Town of Springfield*; NY, *Calendar of New York Colonial Manuscripts*.

8. The American War of Independence: Frontiers of Democracy

176. Ross, *War on the Run*, xvii.
177. Stearns, Whitcher and Parker, *Genealogical and Family History*.
178. Secretary of the Commonwealth of Massachusetts, *Massachusetts Soldiers and Sailors*; NY, *Calendar of Historical Manuscripts*, 99.
179. Nelson, *With Fire and Sword*, 257.
180. Nelson, *With Fire and Sword*, 262; Morrissey, *Boston 1775*, 54, 58.
181. Morrissey, *Boston 1775*, 54–55.
182. Morrissey, *Boston 1775*, 65.
183. Morrissey, *Boston 1775*, 65.
184. Cohen, *Conquered into Liberty*, xi.
185. Ross, *War on the Run*, 421–27.
186. Ross, *War on the Run*, 428–25.

187. Ross, *War on the Run*, 442–50.
188. Ross, *War on the Run*, 442–50.
189. Gabriel, *Battle of Bennington*.
190. Gabriel, *Battle of Bennington*.
191. Cohen, *Conquered into Liberty*, 254.
192. Cohen, *Conquered into Liberty*, 254.
193. Ketchum, *Saratoga*, 287.
194. Hammond, *Rolls of the Soldiers*.
195. Potter, *Military History*, 317–18.
196. Potter, *Military History*, 320.
197. Potter, *Military History*, 318.
198. Cohen, *Conquered into Liberty*, 219.
199. Saunderson, *History of Charlestown*, 589.
200. Locke, *Memorial of Joshua Locke*.
201. Find a Grave, https://www.findagrave.com.
202. Smith, *History of Addison County*, 641–44.
203. Ferrisburgh Town Records.
204. Ferrisburgh Town Records.

9. The War of 1812: The Last Battle for Lake Champlain

205. Johnson, *State of Vermont Roster*; Find a Grave.
206. Daughan, *1812*, 104.
207. Daughan, *1812*, 119.
208. Daughan, *1812*, 181–82.
209. Daughan, *1812*, 183–84.
210. Daughan, *1812*, 183.
211. National Archives, *Pension File 11802, Courtney, James, War of 1812*, fold3.com; National Archives, *Pension File 1367, Sharpe, Reuben (alias Robert Gary), War of 1812*, fold3.com (included in National Archives General References).
212. Daughan, *1812*, 261, 264–65.
213. Crawford, *Naval War of 1812*, 605.
214. Pensions of James Courtney and Reuben Sharpe.
215. Daughan, *1812*, 266.
216. Daughan, *1812*, 266.
217. Crawford, *Naval War of 1812*, 479–83.

218. Smith, *History of Addison County*, xi.
219. Pensions of James Courtney and Reuben Sharpe.
220. Daughan, *1812*, 341–42.
221. Daughan, *1812*, 342–46.
222. Daughan, *1812*, 342–46.
223. Daughan, *1812*, 347.
224. Daughan, *1812*, 347–48.
225. Daughan, *1812*, 349.
226. Pensions of James Courtney and Reuben Sharpe.
227. Daughan, *1812*, 349–50.
228. Pensions of James Courtney and Reuben Sharpe.
229. Daughan, *1812*, 350.
230. Pensions of James Courtney and Reuben Sharpe.
231. Rhode Island, Vital Extracts, 1636–1899, which in turn took it from an 1825 issue of *The Rhode Island American*. Several papers across the Northeast seem to have published the paragraph-long obituary in some form or another. See also headstone transcription from Find a Grave.
232. Niles, *Niles' Weekly Registry*.

BIBLIOGRAPHY

Primary Sources

Bates, Albert C. *Rolls of Connecticut Men in the French & Indian War, 1755–1762*. Vol. 1, *1755–1757*. Connecticut Historical Society, 1903. Internet Archive. https://archive.org.

Church, Thomas, and Samuel G. Drake. *The History of King Philip's War*. Boston: Howe & Norton, 1825. Reprinted by Alpha Editions, 2019.

Dartmouth University. Simon Sartwell deed, Mss 760166. Rauner Library Archives and Manuscripts. https://archives-manuscripts.dartmouth.edu.

Hammond, Isaac W., ed. *Rolls of the Soldiers in the Revolutionary War, May 1777 to 1780: with an Appendix Embracing Names of New Hampshire in Massachusetts Regiments*. Vol. 2. Parsons B. Cogswell, State Printer, 1886.

Heywood, William. "Unpublished Journal." Silsby Free Public Library, Charlestown, New Hampshire.

Holbrook, Jay Mack, ed. *Vermont 1771 Census*. Holbrook Research Institute, 1982.

Johnson, Herbert T., ed. *State of Vermont Roster of Soldiers in the War of 1812–14*. Messenger Press, 1933.

Locke, Joshua. "The Memorial of Joshua Locke." MS.2143. Ticonderoga Online Collections. 1782–1789. https://fortticonderoga.catalogaccess.com/archives/30124.

National Archives. "Pension File 11802, Courtney, James, War of 1812." fold3.com.

———. "Pension File 1367, Sharpe, Reuben (alias Robert Gary), War of 1812."

Niles, H., ed. *Niles' Weekly Registry*. Vol. 28, *March 1825 to September 1825*. Franklin Press, 1825. Google Books.

Rogers, Robert. *Journals of Major Robert Rogers*. London: J. Milan, 1765. Reprint, New York: Corinth Books, 1965.

Secretary of State of New York. *Calendar of Historical Manuscripts relating to the War of the Revolution in the Office of the Secretary of State, Albany, New York*. Vol. 1. Weed, Parsons and Company, 1868. Google Books.

———. *Calendar of N.Y. Colonial Manuscripts, Indorsed Land Papers in the Office of the Secretary of State of New York, 1643–1803*. Weed, Parsons and Company, 1864. Google Books.

Secretary of the Commonwealth of Massachusetts. *Massachusetts Soldiers and Sailors of the Revolutionary War*. Vols. 1–17. Wright & Potter Printing, 1896–1908.

Stark, Caleb. *Memoir and Official Correspondence of Gen. John Stark with Notice of Several Other Officers of the Revolution. Also, a Biography of Captain Phinehas Stevens and of Col. Robert Rogers, with an Account of His Services in America During the "Seven Years War."* Steam Press of McFarland & Jenks, 1860. Google Books.

Town of Charlestown, New Hampshire. Town Records 1753–1900. FamilySearch. https://www.familysearch.org/en/united-states/.

Town of Ferrisburgh, Vermont. Town Records, 1759–1872. FamilySearch. https://www.familysearch.org/en/united-states/.

Town of Springfield, Vermont. Town Records 1769–1842. FamilySearch. https://www.familysearch.org/en/united-states/.

SECONDARY SOURCES

Anderson, Fred. *Crucible of War: The Seven Years War & the Fate of Empire in British North America 1754–1766*. Alfred A. Knopf, 2000.

Borneman, Walter R. *The French and Indian War: Deciding the Fate of North America*. HarperCollins, 2006.

Calloway, Colin G. *The Western Abenakis of Vermont, 1600–1800: War, Migration, and the Survival of an Indian People*. University of Oklahoma Press, 1990.

Chartrand, Rene. *Raiders from New France: North American Forest Warfare Tactics, 17th–18th Centuries*. Osprey Publishing, 2019.

———. *Ticonderoga 1758: Montcalm's Victory Against All Odds*. Osprey Publishing, 2000.

Cohen, Eliot A. *Conquered into Liberty: Two Centuries of Battles along the Great Warpath That Made the American Way of War.* Free Press, 2011.

Connecticut Historical Society. *Papers and Reports Presented to the Connecticut Historical Society at the Annual Meeting of the Society, May 27, 1890.* Connecticut Historical Society, 1890. Google Books.

Crawford, Michael J., ed. *The Naval War of 1812: A Documentary History.* Vol. 3. Naval Historical Center, Department of the Navy, 2002.

Cutter, William Richard, ed. *Historic Homes and Places and Genealogical and Personal Memoirs Relating to the Families of Middlesex County, Massachusetts.* Vol 2. Lewis Historical Publishing Company, 1908. Google Books.

Darby, William O., and William H. Baumer. *Darby's Rangers: We Led the Way.* Presidio Press, 1980.

Daughan, George C. *1812: The Navy's War.* Basic Books, 2011.

Doughty, Sir Arthur, ed. *Appendix to an Historical Journal of the Campaigns in North America For the Years 1757, 1758, 1759, and 1760 by Captain John Knox.* Vol. 3. Champlain Society, 1916. Google Books.

Flavell, Julie. *The Howe Dynasty: The Untold Story of a Military Family and the Women Behind Britain's Wars for America.* Liveright Publishing Corporation, 2021.

Gabriel, Michael P. *The Battle of Bennington: Soldiers & Civilians.* The History Press, 2012.

Gordon, General George A. "The Defense of Fort Number Four (now Charlestown, N.H.) Against the Indians." *The Granite Monthly, A New Hampshire Magazine Devoted to History, Biography, Literature, State Progress.* Monthly Publishing Company, 1908. Google Books.

Hall, Benjamin H. *History of Eastern Vermont: From Its Earliest Settlement to the Close of the Eighteenth Century, With a Biographical Chapter and Appendixes.* D. Appleton & Company, 1858. Google Books.

Hamilton, Edward P. *Fort Ticonderoga, Key to a Continent.* Little, Brown and Company, 1964.

Hubbard, Charles Horace, and Justus Dartt. *History of the Town of Springfield, Vermont, with a Genealogical Record.* George H. Walker and Company, 1895. Google Books.

Johnson, Michael. *Indian Tribes of the New England Frontier.* Osprey Publishing, 2006.

Ketchum, Richard M. *Saratoga: Turning Point of America's Revolutionary War.* Henry Holt & Company, 1997.

Lee, Francis Bazley, ed. *Genealogical and Memorial History of the State of New Jersey.* Vol. 3. Lewis Historical Publishing Company, 1910. Google Books.

Loescher, Burt Garfield. *The History of Rogers Rangers.* Vols. 1–4. Heritage Books, 2001.

MacKay, Robert E. *Massachusetts Soldiers in the French and Indian Wars 1744–1755*. New England Historic Genealogical Society, 1978.

Morrissey, Brendan. *Boston 1775: The Shot Heard Around the World*. Osprey Publishing, 1995.

Nelson, James L. *With Fire and Sword: The Battle of Bunker Hill and the Beginning of the American Revolution*. Thomas Dunne Books, 2011.

Potter, Clarence Eastman. *Military History of the State of New Hampshire*. McFarland & Jenks, 1866.

Richardson, Frederick W. *Eighteenth Century Springfield: From Wilderness to Vermont Statehood, 1751 to 1791*. Newport Litho, 1991.

Ross, John F. *War on the Run: The Epic Story of Robert Rogers and the Conquest of America's First Frontier*. Bantam Books, 2011.

Saunderson, Henry Hamilton. *History of Charlestown, New Hampshire, The Old No. 4*. Forgotten Books, 2018.

Schultz, Eric B., and Michael J. Tougias. *King Philip's War: The History and Legacy of America's Forgotten Conflict*. Countryman Press, 1999.

Smith, H.P., ed. *History of Addison County, Vermont*. D. Mason and Company, 1886. Google Books.

Stachiw, Myron O. *Massachusetts Officers and Soldiers, 1723–1743, Dummer's War to the War of Jenkins Ear*. New England Historic Genealogical Society, 1947.

Stearns, Ezra S., William F. Whitcher and Edward E. Parker, eds. *Genealogical and Family History of the State of New Hampshire*. Lewis Publishing Company, 1908. Google Books.

Stoutenburgh, John, Jr. *Dictionary of the American Indian: An A-to-Z Guide to Indian History, Legend, and Lore*. Philosophical Library, 1960.

Temple, J.H., and George Sheldon. *History of the Town of Northfield, Massachusetts, for 150 Years*. Joel Munsell, 1875. Google Books.

Trumbull, James Russell. *History of Northampton, Massachusetts: From Its Settlement in 1654*. Vol. 1. Gazette Printing Company, 1898. Google Books.

Wells, Frederic P. *History of Newbury, Vermont: From the Discovery of the Coos Country to Present Time, With Genealogical Records of Many Families*. The Caledonian Company, 1902. Google Books.

Zaboly, Gary. *American Colonial Ranger: The Northern Colonies 1724–64*. Osprey Publishing, 2004.

General References

Ancestry | www.ancestry.com
Charlestown, New Hampshire Historical Society | https://charlestown-nh.gov/pages/charlestown-historical-society
Dartmouth | https://home.dartmouth.edu/
FamilySearch | www.familysearch.com
Ferrisburgh Historical Society | www.ferrisburghvt.org
Find a Grave | www.findagrave.com
Fort Ticonderoga | www.fortticonderoga.org
George Washington's Mount Vernon | www.mountvernon.org
Google Books | www.books.google.com
Google Maps | www.google.com/maps
Internet Archive | www.archive.org
Massachusetts, U.S., Town and Vital Records, 1620–1988 | www.ancestry.com
National Archives of Great Britain | www.nationalarchives.gov.uk
National Archives of the United States | www.archives.gov
New York Public Library | www.nypl.org
New York State Archives | www.archives.nysed.gov
Rhode Island, Vital Extracts, 1636–1899 | www.ancestry.com
Vermont, Town Clerk, Town and Vital Records, 1732–2005 | www.familysearch.com
Yale Center for British Art | https://britishart.yale.edu/

INDEX

C

G

H

I

J

K

L

M

N

O

P

Q

R

S

ABOUT THE AUTHOR

Anthony Blasi has explored his fair share of wilderness, from the woods of New England to the rainforests of the Amazon. He is a municipal clerk and a member of several genealogical societies throughout the Northeast. He is a graduate of the University of Maine–Farmington, where he received the Roger Grindle award from the History Department and presented a thesis on the history of genealogy in America. In addition to playing the family historian and perusing headstones, he is a keen miniature wargamer. He lives with his wife and daughter in central Maine.